Andrew Marvell

The Works of
Andrew Marvell

❀

*with an Introduction by Andrew Crozier,
and Bibliography*

Wordsworth Poetry Library

This edition published 1995 by Wordsworth Editions Ltd,
Cumberland House, Crib Street, Ware, Hertfordshire SG12 9ET.

ISBN 1-85326-435-0

Typeset in the UK by Antony Gray.
Printed and bound in Denmark by Nørhaven.

The paper in this book is produced from pure wood
pulp, without the use of chlorine or any other substance
harmful to the environment. The energy used in its
production consists almost entirely of hydroelectricity
and heat generated from waste materials, thereby
conserving fossil fuels and contributing little to the
greenhouse effect.

INTRODUCTION

Andrew Marvell could be numbered, we might suppose, with Alexander Pope's 'mob of gentlemen who wrote with ease' during the reigns of Charles I and Charles II. Pope's phrase is not, in fact, the compliment we might easily take it for (indeed, the word 'mob' should have prompted unease enough to put us on our guard), but a professional's comment on an age of amateurs. Although we might assume those gentlemen to be royalist cavaliers, whereas Marvell – as we see from his panegyrics to Oliver Cromwell – adhered to the other side, Pope's judgement might equally seem to apply to him. Marvell himself published few poems, and acknowledged fewer: the poems which comprise most of the poetry accepted to be by him, and which can in most cases be confidently attributed to him, were published posthumously as his *Miscellaneous Poems* in 1681, three years after his death. This collection appears to have been put together from papers left in his London lodgings, and published as a ploy by his landlady, or servant, to pass herself off as his widow – unsuccessfully, as it turned out. For those so inclined the very survival of the poems on which Marvell's modern reputation chiefly depends can seem to owe much to chance. If so, the survival of his Cromwell poems owes even more to chance, for they were suppressed in all but one or two copies of the book.

But it was as a commonwealth'sman, an upholder of religious toleration, and an opponent of the political advisers of Charles II, that Marvell was known in his day, on the basis of his public life, his skill as a writer of controversial prose, and as an author of anonymously circulated satires on public events in the 1660s and 1670s. This Marvell was cherished well into the nineteenth century, and we find him in Wordsworth's sonnet of 1802 in which he is numbered with other seventeenth-century upholders of liberty.

> Great men have been among us; hands that penned
> And tongues that uttered wisdom – better none:
> The later Sidney, Marvel, Harrington,
> Young Vane, and others who called Milton friend.

Marvell's connection with Milton was widely known from his commendatory poem on *Paradise Lost* (first published in the second edition of 1674), and was of long standing. There survives from 1653 a letter written by Milton which is, in effect, a testimonal on behalf of a young man looking for a government post, in which he describes Marvell as a gentleman 'both by report, and the converse I have had with him, of singular desert for the state to make use of; who also offers himself, if there be any employment for him. His father was the minister of Hull and he has spent four years abroad in Holland, France, Italy and Spain, to very good purpose as I believe, and the gaining of those four languages; besides he is a scholar and well read in the Latin and Greek authors, and no doubt of an approved conversation; for he comes now lately out of the house of the Lord of Fairfax, who was General, where he was entrusted to give some instructions in the languages to the Lady his daughter.' This is a good summary of the known facts of Marvell's early life. He had been tutor to General Fairfax's daughter, Mary, at Nun Appleton House in Yorkshire from 1650 to 1652, and became tutor to Cromwell's ward, William Dutton, in 1653. It was probably as a tutor that he went abroad in the early 1640s, after leaving Cambridge, and so was out of the country for most of the Civil War years. In 1657 he became Latin Secretary to the Council of State (he performed other diplomatic roles in the 1660s), and from 1659 until his death was a member of parliament for Hull. The record is of discreet, conscientious, private and public service. It is understood that as a member of parliament he effectively defended Milton when retribution was exacted on the men associated with the execution of Charles I.

It is commonly supposed that many of the poems in Marvell's *Miscellaneous Poems*, and most of those poems of his which are most admired, were written during his period of rural retirement at General Fairfax's house in Yorkshire, where Fairfax himself had retired after resigning command of the army to Cromwell. 'Upon the Hill and Grove at Billborow' and 'Upon Appleton House', commendatory poems in which his patron's private and public merits are refracted through the properties of his house and estate, self-evidently date from this period, and it is reasonable to associate with them Marvell's other poems on gardens, flowers, grass and fields. Certainly, when they were published in 1681, such poems would have seemed dated, period pieces, as more than one critic has observed. But it can be convenient, as well, to see what may well be Marvell's best poetry as in some way also the genuine article, written in a short space of time preceding his entry into public affairs, as though he then gave up the life of a poet. To do so is a matter of taste as much as judgement, and possibly of false taste, for it allows us to admire as finely poised equivocation the treatment of Charles I and Cromwell in 'An Horation Ode upon Cromwell's Return from Ireland' (dateable to 1650, between Cromwell's Irish and Scottish campaigns) but merely to take note of 'The First Anniversary of the Government under Oliver Cromwell' and 'A Poem upon the Death of Oliver Cromwell', to glance indulgently at the Restoration satires, and to ignore altogether the prose writings. Whereas Pope conveniently ignored the interregnum, this view of Marvell tends to associate him with the pre-Civil War culture of courtliness and grace lamented in 'To His Noble Friend, Mr Richard Lovelace, upon His Poems'.

This is unfortunate, for it deprives us of a possible view of Marvell's consistency, and leaves us surely in something of a quandary when we read the lyric poetry so much admired in the twentieth century. How is it that the speaker – even in 'To His Coy Mistress', ostensibly persuasion to sexual surrender – can remain so calm, so equable in tone while in a state of rapt or intrigued contemplation, so lucid in the exhibition to the understanding of the reader of the complexities of argument and individual plight? It is not a question of what Marvell thought, or where he stood, but rather of how we are able to follow his speakers and recognise an impassioned but disciplined train of thought without a concomitant sense of a dramatised and fully present person speaking. We begin to doubt the basis of our experience of having read Marvell. One way of addressing this difficulty is to see Marvell as primarily a literary poet, writing out of but remaining within his knowledge and experience of the themes and conventions of Renaissance poetry, and it is not difficult to make a start in this direction by detecting affinities with Ben Johnson and John Donne. There is no doubt that Marvell was learned and well read, and used his learning and reading in his poetry (as he did in his controversial prose), but to see these accomplishments as the basis of his lyric poetry is to see the poems as literary exercises, when they are plainly more than that; indeed the doubt that they may be no more than such exercises occurs only when we begin to wonder if we have grasped what we have understood. It is surely the case, rather, that Marvell uses his learning, as well as his wit, and his powers of presentation and argument, to engage with his reader on terms of equality. These are poems to be read in our calm and lucid moments, or to induce those qualities in us by calling into play our own powers of thought.

In his poems about Cromwell, Marvell distinguishes between power and arbitrary personal rule, and the distinction concerns the good of the body politic rather than legitimacy. In the 'Horatian Ode' the things regretted in the poem to Lovelace are more vividly realised in the composure displayed on the scaffold by Charles I, but Marvell passes on, almost without regret himself, to deal with matter of more pressing concern to the republic. In the 'First Anniversary', Cromwell is poised between political wrangling at home and Catholic despotism abroad, but the power he wields represents a nation stabilised by the counterbalancing of contrary interest. The fascination Cromwell had for Marvell is the fascination of power, but for Marvell power is political and calls into question relations between the public and private spheres: they are different but not separate. Politically Marvell appears as a pragmatist interested in the public actions of individuals, concerned for the value of the person but in the recognition that individuals cannot live solely on their own account. He was thus adaptable, as of course were many others who made the transition from serving the Protectorate to serving the restored monarchy, but with a core of consistency. What put him in opposition to government under Charles II were issues of freedom of conscience in religion, and of arbitrary and corrupt conduct of policy. In satires on public events which Marvell is known to have written, but not quite so many as were attributed to him when such writings could be published after the deposition of James II, mock-encomium is used to object to the appropriation by the court of public revenues and, spectacular evidence of this, England's naval humiliation by the Dutch. Corruption at court, and conspicuous consumption, went hand in hand with assertions, in some quarters, that individual conscience should be subservient to royal and ecclesiastical authority, which Marvell opposed in *The Rehersal Transprosed* (1672, Second Part 1673) in a style of *ad hominem* raillery which, we are told, so amused the king that its publisher was able to evade censorship.

Marvell's consistency, therefore, lies in a refusal to be doctrinaire, and what amounts to the recognition that the good cannot be won by force or power of argument. His cast of mind is detached and independent; his public stance involved but non-partisan. This can bring us back to the distinctive and difficult qualities of his lyric poetry. Marvell's imagination, it is invariably noted, is strongly visual. The death of Douglas in 'The Loyal Scot' is realised as an extraordinary emblematic tableau, almost as if he is consumed by the fires of love. In 'To His Coy Mistress', Time's chariot has wings. But in this poem, and in the others in which we catch his distinctive lyric tone, his imagination is perhaps more characteristically kinaesthetic, it registers effort and resistance. Pursuing time is apprehended not as a pictorial emblem (indeed, the speaker cannot see it) but as sound and movement (the beating of its wings), and it is in a hurry. And in an ideally timeless world would not space also be contracted, a lovers' amble take in the Humber and the Ganges? It is a daring conceit to draw these two rivers into a single scene, but the wit would remain illustrative if we did not also know what lovers would do in such circumstances. (She, in fact, is not gathering rosebuds but fine rubies.) The special quality of Marvell's imagination, what we are unprepared for, is his mastery and distribution of kinaesthetic effects, achieved by a frequent use of verbs, carefully chosen and contrasted. The word needed to describe this strenuous exercise of the imagination, I think, is speculative, including its almost forgotten sense (which Marvell would have understood) of looking into things within the mind. Marvell does not affect to speak his mind, or open it for inspection, but draws us into its workings.

Andrew Crozier

FURTHER READING

Chernaik, W. L., *The Poet's Time: Politics and Religion in the Work of Andrew Marvell*, 1983

Donno, E. S., *Andrew Marvell: The Critical Heritage*, 1978

Leishmann, J. B., *The Art of Marvell's Poetry*, 1966

Toliver, H. E., *Marvell's Ironic Vision*, 1965

Wilcher, R., *Andrew Marvell*, 1985

CONTENTS

POEMS

SATIRES

POEMS

Upon the Hill and Grove at Billborow

TO THE LORD FAIRFAX

I
See how the archèd earth does here
Rise in a perfect hemisphere!
The stiffest compass could not strike
A line more circular and like,
Nor softest pencil draw a brow
So equal as this hill does bow;
It seems as for a model laid,
And that the world by it was made.

II
Here learn, ye mountains more unjust,
Which to abrupter greatness thrust,
That do, with your hook-shouldered height,
The earth deform, and heaven fright,
For whose excrescence, ill designed,
Nature must a new centre find,
Learn here those humble steps to tread,
Which to securer glory lead.

III
See what a soft access, and wide,
Lies open to its grassy side,
Nor with the rugged path deters
The feet of breathless travellers;
See then how courteous it ascends,
And all the way it rises, bends,
Nor for itself the height does gain,
But only strives to raise the plain;

IV

Yet thus it all the field commands,
And in unenvied greatness stands,
Discerning further than the cliff
Of heaven-daring Teneriff.
How glad the weary seamen haste,
When they salute it from the mast!
By night, the northern star their way
Directs, and this no less by day.

V

Upon its crest, this mountain grave,
A plume of agèd trees does wave.
No hostile hand durst e'er invade,
With impious steel, the sacred shade;
For something always did appear
Of the GREAT MASTER's terror there,
And men could hear his armour still,
Rattling through all the grove and hill.

VI

Fear of the MASTER, and respect
Of the great nymph, did it protect;
VERA, the nymph, that him inspired,
To whom he often here retired,
And on these oaks engraved her name, –
Such wounds alone these woods became;
But ere he well the barks could part,
'Twas writ already in their heart;

VII

For they, 'tis credible, have sense,
As we, of love and reverence,
And underneath the coarser rind
The genius of the house do bind.
Hence they successes seem to know,
And in their Lord's advancement grow;
But in no memory were seen,
As under this, so straight and green;

VIII

Yet now no farther strive to shoot,
Contented, if they fix their root,
Nor to the wind's uncertain gust
Their prudent heads too far entrust.
Only sometimes a fluttering breeze
Discourses with the breathing trees,
Which in their modest whispers name
Those acts that swelled the cheeks of Fame.

IX

'Much other groves,' say they, 'than these,
And other hills, him once did please.
Through groves of pikes he thundered then,
And mountains raised of dying men.
For all the civic garlands due
To him, our branches are but few;
Nor are our trunks enough to bear
The trophies of one fertile year.'

X

'Tis true, ye trees, nor ever spoke
More certain oracles in oak;
But peace, if you his favour prize!
That courage its own praises flies:
Therefore to your obscurer seats
From his own brightness he retreats;
Nor he the hills, without the groves,
Nor height, but with retirement, loves.

Upon Appleton House

TO MY LORD FAIRFAX

I

Within this sober frame expect
Work of no foreign architect;
That unto caves the quarries drew,
And forests did to pastures hew;
Who, of his great design in pain,
Did for a model vault his brain;
Whose columns should so high be raised,
To arch the brows which on them gazed.

II

Why should, of all things, man, unruled,
Such unproportioned dwellings build?
The beasts are by their dens expressed,
And birds contrive an equal nest;
The low-roofed tortoises do dwell
In cases fit of tortoise-shell;
No creature loves an empty space;
Their bodies measure out their place.

III

But he, superfluously spread,
Demands more room alive than dead;
And in his hollow palace goes,
Where winds, as he, themselves may lose.
What need of all this marble crust,
To impark the wanton mole of dust,
That thinks by breadth the world to unite,
Though the first builders failed in height?

IV

But all things are composèd here,
Like nature, orderly, and near;
In which we the dimensions find
Of that more sober age and mind,
When larger-sizèd men did stoop
To enter at a narrow loop,
As practising, in doors so strait,
To strain themselves through Heaven's gate.

V

And surely, when the after-age
Shall hither come in pilgrimage,
These sacred places to adore,
By VERE and FAIRFAX trod before,
Men will dispute how their extent
Within such dwarfish confines went;
And some will smile at this, as well
As Romulus his bee-like cell.

VI

Humility alone designs
Those short but admirable lines
By which, ungirt and unconstrained,
Things greater are in less contained.
Let others vainly strive to immure
The circle in the quadrature!
These holy mathematics can
In every figure equal man.

VII

Yet thus the laden house does sweat,
And scarce endures the master great:
But, where he comes, the swelling hall
Stirs, and the square grows spherical;
More by his magnitude distressed,
Than he is by its straitness pressed:
And too officiously it slights
That in itself, which him delights.

VIII

So honour better lowness bears,
Than that unwonted greatness wears;
Height with a certain grace does bend,
But low things clownishly ascend.
And yet what needs there here excuse,
Where everything does answer use?
Where neatness nothing can condemn,
Nor pride invent what to contemn?

IX

A stately frontispiece of poor
Adorns without the open door;
Nor less the rooms within commends
Daily new furniture of friends.
The house was built upon the place,
Only as for a mark of grace,
And for an inn to entertain
Its Lord awhile, but not remain.

X

Him Bishop's Hill or Denton may,
Or Billborow, better hold than they:
But Nature here hath been so free,
As if she said, 'Leave this to me.'
Art would more neatly have defaced
What she had laid so sweetly waste
In fragrant gardens, shady woods,
Deep meadows, and transparent floods.

XI

While, with slow eyes, we these survey,
And on each pleasant footstep stay,
We opportunely may relate
The progress of this house's fate.
A nunnery first gave it birth,
(For virgin buildings oft brought forth,)
And all that neighbour-ruin shows
The quarries whence this dwelling rose.

XII

Near to this gloomy cloister's gates
There dwelt the blooming virgin THWAITES,
Fair beyond measure, and an heir,
Which might deformity make fair;
And oft she spent the summer's suns
Discoursing with the subtle nuns;
Whence, in these words, one to her weaved,
As 'twere by chance, thoughts long conceived:

XIII

'Within this holy leisure, we
Live innocently, as you see.
These walls restrain the world without,
But hedge our liberty about;
These bars inclose that wider den
Of those wild creatures, callèd men;
The cloister outward shuts its gates,
And, from us, locks on them the grates.

XIV

Here we, in shining armour white,
Like virgin amazons do fight,
And our chaste lamps we hourly trim,
Lest the great bridegroom find them dim.
Our orient breaths perfumèd are
With incense of incessant prayer;
And holy-water of our tears
Most strangely our complexion clears;

XV

Not tears of grief, but such as those
With which calm pleasure overflows,
Or pity, when we look on you
That live without this happy vow.
How should we grieve that must be seen,
Each one a spouse, and each a queen;
And can in heaven hence behold
Our brighter robes and crowns of gold!

XVI

When we have prayèd all our beads,
Some one the holy legend reads,
While all the rest with needles paint
The face and graces of the Saint;
But what the linen can't receive,
They in their lives do interweave.
This work the Saints best represents,
That serves for altar's ornaments.

XVII

But much it to our work would add,
If here your hand, your face, we had:
By it we would our Lady touch;
Yet thus she you resembles much.
Some of your features, as we sewed,
Through every shrine should be bestowed,
And in one beauty we would take
Enough a thousand Saints to make.

XVIII

And (for I dare not quench the fire
That me does for your good inspire)
'Twere sacrilege a man to admit
To holy things, for heaven fit.
I see the angels, in a crown,
On you the lilies showering down;
And round about you, glory breaks,
That something more than human speaks.

XIX

All beauty when at such a height
Is so already consecrate.
FAIRFAX I know, and long ere this
Have marked the youth, and what he is;
But can he such a rival seem,
For whom you Heaven should disesteem?
Ah, no! and 'twould more honour prove
He your devoto were than love.

XX

Here live belovèd and obeyed,
Each one your sister, each your maid,
And, if our rule seemed strictly penned,
The rule itself to you shall bend.
Our Abbess, too, now far in age,
Doth your succession near presage.
How soft the yoke on us would lie
Might such fair hands as yours it tie

XXI

Your voice, the sweetest of the choir,
Shall draw heaven nearer, raise us higher,
And your example, if our head,
Will soon us to perfection lead.
Those virtues to us all so dear,
Will straight grow sanctity when here;
And that, once sprung, increase so fast,
Till miracles it work at last.

XXII

Nor is our order yet so nice,
Delight to banish as a vice:
Here Pleasure Piety doth meet,
One perfecting the other sweet;
So through the mortal fruit we boil
The sugar's uncorrupting oil,
And that which perished while we pull,
Is thus preservèd clear and full.

XXIII

For such indeed are all our arts,
Still handling Nature's finest parts:
Flowers dress the altars; for the clothes
The sea-born amber we compose;
Balms for the grieved we draw; and pastes
We mould as baits for curious tastes.
What need is here of man, unless
These as sweet sins we should confess?

XXIV

Each night among us to your side
Appoint a fresh and virgin bride,
Whom, if our Lord at midnight find,
Yet neither should be left behind!
Where you may lie as chaste in bed
As pearls together billeted;
All night embracing, arm in arm,
Like crystal pure, with cotton warm.

XXV

But what is this to all the store
Of joys you see, and may make more?
Try but awhile, if you be wise:
The trial neither costs nor ties.'
Now, FAIRFAX, seek her promised faith;
Religion that dispensèd hath,
Which she henceforward does begin;
The nun's smooth tongue has sucked her in.

XXVI

Oft, though he knew it was in vain,
Yet would he valiantly complain:
'Is this that sanctity so great,
An art by which you finelier cheat?
Hypocrite, witches, hence avaunt,
Who, though in prison, yet enchant!
Death only can such thieves make fast,
As rob, though in the dungeon cast.

XXVII

Were there but, when this house was made,
One stone that a just hand had laid,
It must have fallen upon her head
Who first thee from thy faith misled.
And yet, how well soever meant,
With them 'twould soon grow fraudulent;
For like themselves they alter all,
And vice infects the very wall;

XXVIII

But sure those buildings last not long,
Founded by folly, kept by wrong.
I know what fruit their gardens yield,
When they it think by night concealed.
Fly from their vices: 'tis thy state,
Not thee, that they would consecrate.
Fly from their ruin: how I fear,
Though guiltless, lest thou perish there!'

XXIX

What should he do? He would respect
Religion, but not right neglect:
For first, religion taught him right,
And dazzled not, but cleared his sight.
Sometimes, resolved, his sword he draws,
But reverenceth then the laws;
For justice still that courage led,
First from a judge, then soldier bred.

XXX

Small honour would be in the storm;
The court him grants the lawful form,
Which licensed either peace or force,
To hinder the unjust divorce.
Yet still the nuns his right debarred,
Standing upon their holy guard.
Ill-counselled women, do you know
Whom you resist, or what you do?

XXXI

Is not this he, whose offspring fierce
Shall fight through all the universe;
And with successive valour try
France, Poland, either Germany,
Till one, as long since prophesied,
His horse through conquered Britain ride?
Yet, against fate, his spouse they kept,
And the great race would intercept.

XXXII

Some to the breach, against their foes,
Their wooden Saints in vain oppose;
Another, bolder, stands at push,
With their old holy-water brush;
While the disjointed Abbess threads
The jingling chain-shot of her beads;
But their loud'st cannon were their lungs,
And sharpest weapons were their tongues.

XXXIII

But, waving these aside like flies,
Young FAIRFAX through the wall does rise.
Then the unfrequented vault appeared,
And superstitions, vainly feared;
The relics false were set to view;
Only the jewels there were true;
But truly bright and holy THWAITES,
That weeping at the altar waits.

XXXIV

But the glad youth away her bears,
And to the nuns bequeathes her tears,
Who guiltily their prize bemoan,
Like gipsies that a child have stolen.
Thenceforth (as, when the enchantment ends,
The castle vanishes or rends)
The wasting cloister, with the rest,
Was, in one instant, dispossessed.

XXXV

At the demolishing, this seat
To FAIRFAX fell, as by escheat;
And what both nuns and founders willed,
'Tis likely better thus fulfilled.
For if the virgin proved not theirs,
The cloister yet remainèd hers;
Though many a nun there made her vow,
'Twas no religious house till now.

XXXVI

From that blest bed the hero came
Whom France and Poland yet does fame;
Who, when retirèd here to peace,
His warlike studies could not cease.
But laid these gardens out in sport
In the just figure of a fort,
And with five bastions it did fence,
As aiming one for every sense.

XXXVII

When in the east the morning ray
Hangs out the colours of the day,
The bee through these known alleys hums,
Beating the dian with its drums.
Then flowers their drowsy eyelids raise,
Their silken ensigns each displays,
And dries its pan yet dank with dew,
And fills its flask with odours new.

XXXVIII

These, as their Governor goes by,
In fragrant volleys they let fly,
And to salute their Governess
Again as great a charge they press:
None for the virgin nymph; for she
Seems with the flowers, a flower to be.
And think so still! though not compare
With breath so sweet, or cheek so fair!

XXXIX

Well shot, ye firemen! Oh how sweet
And round your equal fires do meet;
Whose shrill report no ear can tell,
But echoes to the eye and smell!
See how the flowers, as at parade,
Under their colours stand displayed;
Each regiment in order grows,
That of the tulip, pink, and rose.

XL

But when the vigilant patrol
Of stars walks round about the pole,
Their leaves that to the stalks are curled
Seem to their staves the ensigns furled.
Then in some flower's belovèd hut,
Each bee, as sentinel, is shut,
And sleeps so too, but, if once stirred,
She runs you through, nor asks the word.

XLI

Oh thou, that dear and happy isle,
The garden of the world erewhile,
Thou Paradise of the four seas,
Which Heaven planted us to please,
But, to exclude the world, did guard
With watery, if not flaming sword, —
What luckless apple did we taste,
To make us mortal, and thee waste?

XLII

Unhappy! shall we never more
That sweet militia restore,
When gardens only had their towers
And all the garrisons were flowers;
When roses only arms might bear,
And men did rosy garlands wear?
Tulips, in several colours barred,
Were then the Switzers of our guard;

XLIII

The gardener had the soldier's place,
And his more gentle forts did trace;
The nursery of all things green
Was then the only magazine;
The winter quarters were the stoves,
Where he the tender plants removes.
But war all this doth overgrow:
We ordnance plant, and powder sow.

XLIV

And yet there walks one on the sod,
Who, had it pleasèd him and God,
Might once have made our gardens spring
Fresh as his own, and flourishing.
But he preferred to the Cinque Ports
These five imaginary forts,
And, in those half-dry trenches, spanned
Power which the ocean might command.

XLV

For he did, with his utmost skill,
Ambition weed, but conscience till;
Conscience, that heaven-nursèd plant,
Which most our earthly gardens want.
A prickling leaf it bears, and such
As that which shrinks at every touch,
But flowers eternal, and divine,
That in the crowns of Saints do shine.

XLVI

The sight does from these bastions ply,
The invisible artillery,
And at proud Cawood Castle seems
To point the battery of its beams;
As if it quarrelled in the seat,
The ambition of its prelate great;
But o'er the meads below it plays,
Or innocently seems to gaze.

XLVII

And now to the abyss I pass
Of that unfathomable grass,
Where men like grasshoppers appear,
But grasshoppers are giants there:
They, in their squeaking laugh, contemn
Us as we walk more low than them,
And from the precipices tall
Of the green spires to us do call.

XLVIII

To see men through this meadow dive,
We wonder how they rise alive;
As, under water, none does know
Whether he fall through it or go;
But, as the mariners that sound,
And show upon their lead the ground,
They bring up flowers so to be seen,
And prove they've at the bottom been.

XLIX

No scene, that turns with engines strange,
Does oftener than these meadows change;
For when the sun the grass hath vexed,
The tawny mowers enter next,
Who seem like Israelites to be
Walking on foot through a green sea.
To them the grassy deeps divide,
And crowd a lane to either side;

L

With whistling scythe and elbow strong
These massacre the grass along,
While one, unknowing, carves the rail,
Whose yet unfeathered quills her fail;
The edge all bloody from its breast
He draws, and does his stroke detest,
Fearing the flesh, untimely mowed,
To him a fate as black forebode.

LI

But bloody Thestylis, that waits
To bring the mowing camp their cates,
Greedy as kite, has trussed it up
And forthwith means on it to sup;
When on another quick she lights,
And cries, 'He called us Israelites;
But now, to make his saying true,
Rails rain for quails, for manna dew.'

LII

Únhappy birds! what does it boot
To build below the grass's root;
When lowness is unsafe as height,
And chance o'ertakes what 'scapeth spite?
And now your orphan parent's call
Sounds your untimely funeral;
Death-trumpets creak in such a note,
And 'tis the sourdine in their throat.

LIII

Or sooner hatch, or higher build;
The mower now commands the field,
In whose new traverse seemeth wrought
A camp of battle newly fought,
Where, as the meads with hay, the plain
Lies quilted o'er with bodies slain:
The women that with forks it fling
Do represent the pillaging.

LIV

And now the careless victors play,
Dancing the triumphs of the hay,
Where every mower's wholesome heat
Smells like an ALEXANDER's sweat;
Their females fragrant as the mead
Which they in fairy circles tread:
When at their dance's end they kiss,
Their new-made hay not sweeter is;

LV

When, after this, 'tis piled in cocks,
Like a calm sea it shews the rocks,
We wondering in the river near
How boats among them safely steer;
Or, like the desert Memphis' sand,
Short pyramids of hay do stand;
And such the Roman camps do rise
In hills for soldiers' obsequies.

LVI

This scene, again withdrawing, brings
A new and empty face of things;
A levelled space, as smooth and plain,
As clothes for LILLY stretched to stain.
The world when first created sure
Was such a table rase and pure;
Or rather such is the Toril,
Ere the bulls enter at Madril;

LVII

For to this naked equal flat,
Which levellers take pattern at,
The villagers in common chase
Their cattle, which it closer rase;
And what below the scythe increased
Is pinched yet nearer by the beast.
Such, in the painted world, appeared
Davenant, with the universal herd.

LVIII

They seem within the polished grass
A landscape drawn in looking-glass;
And shrunk in the huge pasture, show
As spots, so shaped, on faces do;
Such fleas, ere they approach the eye,
In multiplying glasses lie.
They feed so wide, so slowly move,
As constellations do above.

LIX

Then, to conclude these pleasant acts,
Denton sets ope its cataracts;
And makes the meadow truly be
(What it but seemed before) a sea;
For, jealous of its Lord's long stay,
It tries to invite him thus away.
The river in itself is drowned,
And isles the astonished cattle round.

LX

Let others tell the paradox,
How eels now bellow in the ox;
How horses at their tails do kick,
Turned, as they hang, to leeches quick;
How boats can over bridges sail,
And fishes do the stables scale;
How salmons trespassing are found,
And pikes are taken in the pound;

LXI

But I, retiring from the flood,
Take sanctuary in the wood;
And, while it lasts, myself embark
In this yet green, yet growing ark,
Where the first carpenter might best
Fit timber for his keel have pressed,
And where all creatures might have shares,
Although in armies, not in pairs.

LXII

The double wood, of ancient stocks,
Linked in so thick an union locks,
It like two pedigrees appears,
On one hand FAIRFAX, th'other VERES:
Of whom though many fell in war,
Yet more to Heaven shooting are:
And, as they Nature's cradle decked,
Will, in green age, her hearse expect.

LXIII

When first the eye this forest sees,
It seems indeed as wood, not trees;
As if their neighbourhood so old
To one great trunk them all did mould.
There the huge bulk takes place, as meant
To thrust up a fifth element,
And stretches still so closely wedged,
As if the night within were hedged.

LXIV

Dark all without it knits; within
It opens passable and thin,
And in as loose an order grows,
As the Corinthian porticos.
The arching boughs unite between
The columns of the temple green,
And underneath the wingèd quires
Echo about their tunèd fires.

LXV

The nightingale does here make choice
To sing the trials of her voice;
Low shrubs she sits in, and adorns
With music high the squatted thorns;
But highest oaks stoop down to hear,
And listening elders prick the ear;
The thorn, lest it should hurt her, draws
Within the skin its shrunken claws.

LXVI

But I have for my music found
A sadder, yet more pleasing sound;
The stock-doves, whose fair necks are graced
With nuptial rings, their ensigns chaste;
Yet always, for some cause unknown,
Sad pair, unto the elms they moan.
O why should such a couple mourn,
That in so equal flames do burn!

LXVII

Then as I careless on the bed
Of gelid strawberries do tread,
And through the hazels thick espy
The hatching throstle's shining eye,
The heron, from the ash's top,
The eldest of its young lets drop,
As if it stork-like did pretend
That tribute to its Lord to send.

LXVIII

But most the hewel's wonders are,
Who here as the holtfelster's care;
He walks still upright from the root,
Measuring the timber with his foot,
And all the way, to keep it clean,
Doth from the bark the wood-moths glean;
He, with his beak, examines well
Which fit to stand, and which to fell;

LXIX

The good he numbers up, and hacks
As if he marked them with the axe;
But where he, tinkling with his beak,
Does find the hollow oak to speak,
That for his building he designs,
And through the tainted side he mines.
Who could have thought the tallest oak
Should fall by such a feeble stroke?

LXX

Nor would it, had the tree not fed
A traitor worm, within it bred,
(As first our flesh, corrupt within,
Tempts impotent and bashful sin,)
And yet that worm triumphs not long,
But serves to feed the hewel's young,
While the oak seems to fall content,
Viewing the treason's punishment.

LXXI

Thus, I, easy philosopher,
Among the birds and trees confer;
And little now to make me wants
Or of the fowls, or of the plants:
Give me but wings as they, and I
Straight floating on the air shall fly;
Or turn me but, and you shall see
I was but an inverted tree.

LXXII

Already I begin to call
In their most learned original,
And, where I language want, my signs
The bird upon the bough divines,
And more attentive there doth sit
Than if she were with lime-twigs knit.
No leaf does tremble in the wind,
Which I returning cannot find;

LXXIII

Out of these scattered Sibyls' leaves
Strange prophecies my fancy weaves,
And in one history consumes,
Like Mexique paintings, all the plumes;
What Rome, Greece, Palestine, e'er said,
I in this light mosaic read.
Thrice happy he, who, not mistook,
Hath read in Nature's mystic book!

LXXIV

And see how chances better wit
Could with a mask my studies hit!
The oak-leaves me embroider all,
Between which caterpillars crawl;
And ivy, with familiar trails,
Me licks and clasps, and curls and hales.
Under this antic cope I move,
Like some great prelate of the grove;

LXXV

Then, languishing with ease, I toss
On pallets swollen of velvet moss,
While the wind, cooling through the boughs,
Flatters with air my panting brows.
Thanks for my rest, ye mossy banks,
And unto you, cool zephyrs, thanks,
Who, as my hair, my thoughts too shed,
And winnow from the chaff my head!

LXXVI

How safe, methinks, and strong behind
These trees, have I encamped my mind;
Where beauty, aiming at the heart,
Bends in some tree its useless dart,
And where the world no certain shot
Can make, or me it toucheth not,
But I on it securely play,
And gall its horsemen all the day.

LXXVII

Bind me, ye woodbines, in your twines;
Curl me about, ye gadding vines;
And oh, so close your circles lace,
That I may never leave this place!
But, lest your fetters prove too weak,
Ere I your silken bondage break,
Do you, O brambles, chain me too,
And, courteous briars, nail me through!

LXXVIII

Here in the morning tie my chain,
Where the two woods have made a lane,
While, like a guard on either side,
The trees before their Lord divide;
This, like a long and equal thread,
Betwixt two labyrinths does lead.
But, where the floods did lately drown,
There at the evening stake me down;

LXXIX

For now the waves are fallen and dried,
And now the meadows fresher dyed,
Whose grass, with moisture colour dashed,
Seems as green silks but newly washed.
No serpent new, nor crocodile,
Remains behind our little Nile;
Unless itself you will mistake
Among these meads the only snake.

LXXX

See in what wanton harmless folds
It everywhere the meadow holds,
And its yet muddy back doth lick,
Till as a crystal mirror slick,
Where all things gaze themselves, and doubt
If they be in it, or without;
And for his shade which therein shines,
Narcissus-like, the sun too pines.

LXXXI

Oh what a pleasure 'tis to hedge
My temples here with heavy sedge;
Abandoning my lazy side,
Stretched as a bank unto the tide;
Or to suspend my sliding foot
On the osier's underminèd root,
And in its branches tough to hang,
While at my lines the fishes twang!

LXXXII

But now away my hooks, my quills,
And angles, idle utensils!
The young MARIA walks to-night:
Hide, trifling youth, thy pleasures slight;
'Twere shame that such judicious eyes
Should with such toys a man surprise;
She that already is the law
Of all her sex, her age's awe.

LXXXIII

See how loose Nature, in respect
To her, itself doth recollect,
And every thing so whisht and fine,
Starts forthwith into its *bonne mine.*
The sun himself of her aware,
Seems to descend with greater care,
And, lest she see him go to bed,
In blushing clouds conceals his head.

LXXXIV

So when the shadows laid asleep,
From underneath these banks do creep,
And on the river, as it flows,
With ebon shuts begin to close,
The modest halcyon comes in sight,
Flying betwixt the day and night;
And such a horror calm and dumb,
Admiring Nature does benumb;

LXXXV

The viscous air, wheres'er she fly,
Follows and sucks her azure dye;
The jellying stream compacts below,
If it might fix her shadow so;
The stupid fishes hang, as plain
As flies in crystal overta'en.
And men the silent scene assist,
Charmed with the sapphire-wingèd mist.

LXXXVI

MARIA such, and so doth hush
The world, and through the evening rush.
No new-born comet such a train
Draws through the sky, nor star new slain.
For straight those giddy rockets fail,
Which from the putrid earth exhale;
But by her flames, in Heaven tried,
Nature is wholly vitrified.

LXXXVII

'Tis she that to these gardens gave
That wondrous beauty which they have;
She straightness on the woods bestows;
To her the meadow sweetness owes;
Nothing could make the river be
So crystal pure, but only she,
She yet more pure, sweet, straight, and fair
Than gardens, woods, meads, rivers are.

LXXXVIII

Therefore what first she on them spent,
They gratefully again present;
The meadow carpets where to tread,
The garden flowers to crown her head,
And for a glass the limpid brook,
Where she may all her beauties look;
But, since she would not have them seen,
The wood about her draws a screen.

LXXXIX

For she to higher beauties raised,
Disdains to be for lesser praised.
She counts her beauty to converse
In all the languages as hers;
Nor yet in those herself employs,
But for the wisdom, not the noise;
Nor yet that wisdom would affect,
But as 'tis Heaven's dialect.

LXXXX

Blest nymph! that couldst so soon prevent
Those trains by youth against thee meant;
Tears (watery shot that pierce the mind,)
And sighs (Love's cannon charged with wind;)
True praise (that breaks through all defence,)
And feigned complying innocence;
But knowing where this ambush lay,
She 'scaped the safe, but roughest way.

LXXXXI

This 'tis to have been from the first
In a domestic Heaven nursed,
Under the discipline severe
Of FAIRFAX, and the starry VERE;
Where not one object can come nigh
But pure, and spotless as the eye,
And goodness doth itself entail
On females, if there want a male.

LXXXXII

Go now fond sex, that on your face
Do all your useless study place,
Nor once at vice your brows dare knit,
Lest the smooth forehead wrinkled sit:
Yet your own face shall at you grin,
Thorough the black bag of your skin;
When knowledge only could have filled,
And virtue all those furrows tilled.

LXXXXIII

Hence she with graces more divine
Supplies beyond her sex the line;
And, like a sprig of mistletoe,
On the Fairfacian oak does grow;
Whence, for some universal good,
The priest shall cut the sacred bud;
While her glad parents most rejoice
And make their destiny their choice.

LXXXXIV

Meantime, ye fields, springs, bushes, flowers,
Where yet she leads her studious hours,
(Till Fate her worthily translates
And find a FAIRFAX for our THWAITES,)
Employ the means you have by her,
And in your kind yourselves prefer;
That, as all virgins she precedes,
So you all woods, streams, gardens, meads.

LXXXXV

For you, Thessalian Tempe's seat
Shall now be scorned as obsolete;
Aranjuez, as less, disdained;
The Bel-Retiro, as constrained;
But name not the Idalian grove,
For 'twas the seat of wanton love;
Much less the dead's Elysian fields;
Yet nor to them your beauty yields.

LXXXXVI

'Tis not, as once appeared the world,
A heap confused together hurled;
All negligently overthrown,
Gulfs, deserts, precipices, stone;
Your lesser world contains the same,
But in more decent order tame;
You, Heaven's centre, Nature's lap;
And Paradise's only map.

LXXXXVII

And now the salmon-fishers moist
Their leathern boats begin to hoist;
And, like Antipodes in shoes,
Have shod their heads in their canoes.
How tortoise-like, but not so slow,
These rational amphibii go!
Let's in; for the dark hemisphere
Does now like one of them appear.

The Coronet

When for the thorns with which I long, too long,
      With many a piercing wound,
       My Saviour's head have crowned,
I seek with garlands to redress that wrong, –
      Through every garden, every mead,
I gather flowers (my fruits are only flowers),
      Dismantling all the fragrant towers
That once adorned my shepherdess's head:
And now, when I have summed up all my store,
      Thinking (so I myself deceive)
      So rich a chaplet thence to weave
As never yet the King of Glory wore,
      Alas! I find the Serpent old,
      That, twining in his speckled breast,
      About the flowers disguised, does fold
      With wreaths of fame and interest.
Ah, foolish man, that wouldst debase with them,
And mortal glory, Heaven's diadem!
But thou who only couldst the Serpent tame,
Either his slippery knots at once untie,
And disentangle all his winding snare,
Or shatter too with him my curious frame,
And let these wither – so that he may die –
Though set with skill, and chosen out with care;
That they, while thou on both their spoils dost tread,
May crown Thy feet, that could not crown Thy head.

Eyes and Tears

I

How wisely Nature did decree,
With the same eyes to weep and see;
That, having viewed the object vain,
They might be ready to complain!

II

And, since the self-deluding sight
In a false angle takes each height,
These tears, which better measure all,
Like watery lines and plummets fall.

III

Two tears, which sorrow long did weigh
Within the scales of either eye,
And then paid out in equal poise,
Are the true price of all my joys.

IV

What in the world most fair appears,
Yea, even laughter, turns to tears;
And all the jewels which we prize
Melt in these pendants of the eyes.

V

I have through every garden been,
Amongst the red, the white, the green,
And yet from all the flowers I saw,
No honey, but these tears could draw.

VI

So the all-seeing sun each day
Distils the world with chymic ray;
But finds the essence only showers,
Which straight in pity back he pours.

VII

Yet happy they whom grief doth bless,
That weep the more, and see the less;
And, to preserve their sight more true,
Bathe still their eyes in their own dew.

VIII

So Magdalen in tears more wise
Dissolved those captivating eyes,
Whose liquid chains could flowing meet
To fetter her Redeemer's feet.

IX

Not full sails hasting loaden home,
Nor the chaste lady's pregnant womb,
Nor Cynthia teeming shows so fair
As two eyes swollen with weeping are.

X

The sparkling glance that shoots desire
Drenched in these waves, does lose its fire;
Yea oft the Thunderer pity takes,
And here the hissing lightning slakes.

XI

The incense was to Heaven dear,
Not as a perfume, but a tear;
And stars shew lovely in the night,
But as they seem the tears of light.

XII

Ope then, mine eyes, your double sluice,
And practise so your noblest use;
For others too can see, or sleep,
But only human eyes can weep.

XIII

Now, like two clouds dissolving, drop,
And at each tear, in distance stop;
Now, like two fountains, trickle down;
Now, like two floods, o'erturn and drown:

XIV

Thus let your streams o'erflow your springs,
Till eyes and tears be the same things;
And each the other's difference bears,
These weeping eyes, those seeing tears.

Bermudas

Where the remote Bermudas ride,
In the ocean's bosom unespied,
From a small boat, that rowed along,
The listening winds received this song:

'What should we do but sing His praise,
That led us through the watery maze,
Unto an isle so long unknown,
And yet far kinder than our own?
Where He the huge sea-monsters wracks,
That lift the deep upon their backs;
He lands us on a grassy stage,
Safe from the storms, and prelate's rage.
He gave us this eternal spring,
Which here enamels every thing,
And sends the fowls to us in care,
On daily visits through the air;
He hangs in shades the orange bright,
Like golden lamps in a green night,
And does in the pomegranates close
Jewels more rich than Ormus shows;
He makes the figs our mouths to meet,
And throws the melons at our feet;

But apples plants of such a price,
No tree could ever bear them twice;
With cedars chosen by His hand,
From Lebanon, He stores the land,
And makes the hollow seas, that roar,
Proclaim the ambergris on shore;
He cast (of which we rather boast)
The Gospel's pearl upon our coast,
And in these rocks for us did frame
A temple where to sound His name.
Oh! let our voice His praise exalt,
Till it arrive at Heaven's vault,
Which, thence (perhaps) rebounding, may
Echo beyond the Mexique Bay.'

Thus sung they, in the English boat,
An holy and a cheerful note;
And all the way, to guide their chime,
With falling oars they kept the time.

Clorinda and Damon

Clorinda   Damon, come drive thy flocks this way.

Damon   No: 'tis too late they went astray.

Clorinda   I have a grassy scutcheon spied,
Where Flora blazons all her pride;
The grass I aim to feast thy sheep,
The flowers I for thy temples keep.

Damon   Grass withers, and the flowers too fade.

Clorinda   Seize the short joys then, ere they vade.
Seest thou that unfrequented cave?

Damon   That den?

Clorinda   Love's shrine.

Damon	But virtue's grave.
Clorinda	In whose cool bosom we may lie, Safe from the sun.
Damon	Not Heaven's eye.
Clorinda	Near this, a fountain's liquid bell Tinkles within the concave shell.
Damon	Might a soul bathe there and be clean, Or slake its drought?
Clorinda	What is't you mean?
Damon	These once had been enticing things, Clorinda, pastures, caves, and springs.
Clorinda	And what late change?
Damon	The other day Pan met me.
Clorinda	What did great Pan say?
Damon	Words that transcend poor shepherd's skill; But he e'er since my songs does fill, And his name swells my slender oat.
Clorinda	Sweet must Pan sound in Damon's note.
Damon	Clorinda's voice might make it sweet.
Clorinda	Who would not in Pan's praises meet?
Chorus	Of Pan the flowery pastures sing, Caves echo, and the fountains ring. Sing then while he doth us inspire; For all the world is our Pan's quire.

A Dialogue between the Soul and Body

Soul   O, who shall from this dungeon raise
A soul enslaved so many ways?
With bolts of bones, that fettered stands
In feet, and manacled in hands;
Here blinded with an eye, and there
Deaf with the drumming of an ear;
A soul hung up, as 'twere, in chains
Of nerves, and arteries, and veins;
Tortured, besides each other part,
In a vain head, and double heart?

Body   O who shall me deliver whole
From bonds of this tyrannic soul?
Which, stretched upright, impales me so
That mine own precipice I go;
And warms and moves this needless frame,
(A fever could but do the same,)
And, wanting where its spite to try,
Has made me live to let me die
A body that could never rest
Since this ill spirit it possessed.

Soul   What magic could me thus confine
Within another's grief to pine?
Where, whatsoever it complain,
I feel, that cannot feel, the pain;
And all my care itself employs,
That to preserve which me destroys;
Constrained not only to endure
Diseases, but, what's worse, the cure;
And, ready oft the port to gain,
Am shipwrecked into health again.

Body   But Physic yet could never reach
The maladies thou me dost teach;
Whom first the cramp of hope does tear,
And then the palsy shakes of fear;

The pestilence of love does heat,
Or hatred's hidden ulcer eat;
Joy's cheerful madness does perplex,
Or sorrow's other madness vex;
Which knowledge forces me to know,
And memory will not forego;
What but a soul could have the wit
To build me up for sin so fit?
So architects do square and hew
Green trees that in the forest grew.

A Dialogue between the Resolved Soul and Created Pleasure

Courage, my soul! now learn to wield
The weight of thine immortal shield;
Close on thy head thy helmet bright;
Balance thy sword against the fight;
See where an army, strong as fair,
With silken banners spreads the air!
Now, if thou be'st that thing divine,
In this day's combat let it shine,
And show that Nature wants an art
To conquer one resolvèd heart.

Pleasure   Welcome the creation's guest,
Lord of earth, and Heaven's heir!
Lay aside that warlike crest,
And of Nature's banquet share;
Where the souls of fruits and flowers
Stand prepared to heighten yours.

Soul   I sup above, and cannot stay,
To bait so long upon the way.

Pleasure   On these downy pillows lie,
Whose soft plumes will thither fly:

On these roses, strowed so plain
Lest one leaf thy side should strain.

Soul   My gentler rest is on a thought,
Conscious of doing what I ought.

Pleasure If thou be'st with perfumes pleased,
Such as oft the gods appeased,
Thou in fragrant clouds shalt show,
Like another god below.

Soul   A soul that knows not to presume,
Is Heaven's, and its own, perfume.

Pleasure Everything does seem to vie
Which should first attract thine eye:
But since none deserves that grace,
In this crystal view thy face.

Soul   When the Creator's skill is prized,
The rest is all but earth disguised.

Pleasure Hark how music then prepares
For thy stay these charming airs,
Which the posting winds recall,
And suspend the river's fall.

Soul   Had I but any time to lose,
On this I would it all dispose.
Cease, tempter! None can chain a mind,
Whom this sweet cordage cannot bind.

Chorus   Earth cannot show so brave a sight,
As when a single soul does fence
The batteries of alluring sense,
And Heaven views it with delight.
Then persevere; for still new charges sound,
And if thou overcom'st thou shalt be crowned.

Pleasure All that's costly, fair, and sweet,
Which scatteringly doth shine,
Shall within one beauty meet,
And she be only thine.

Soul   If things of sight such heavens be,
              What heavens are those we cannot see?

Pleasure   Wheresoe'er thy foot shall go
                  The minted gold shall lie,
              Till thou purchase all below,
                  And want new worlds to buy.

Soul   We'rt not for price who'd value gold?
              And that's worth naught that can be sold.

Pleasure   Wilt thou all the glory have
                  That war or peace commend?
              Half the world shall be thy slave,
                  The other half thy friend.

Soul   What friend, if to myself untrue?
              What slaves, unless I captive you?

Pleasure   Thou shalt know each hidden cause,
                  And see the future time;
              Try what depth the centre draws,
                  And then to Heaven climb.

Soul   None thither mounts by the degree
              Of knowledge, but humility.

Chorus   Triumph, triumph, victorious soul!
                  The world has not one pleasure more:
              The rest does lie beyond the pole,
                  And is thine everlasting store.

The Nymph Complaining for the Death of Her Fawn

The wanton troopers riding by
Have shot my fawn, and it will die.
Ungentle men! they cannot thrive
Who killed thee. Thou ne'er didst alive
Them any harm, alas! nor could
Thy death yet do them any good.
I'm sure I never wished them ill;
Nor do I for all this, nor will:
But, if my simple prayers may yet
Prevail with Heaven to forget
Thy murder, I will join my tears,
Rather than fail. But, O my fears!
It cannot die so. Heaven's king
Keeps register of everything,
And nothing may we use in vain;
Even beasts must be with justice slain,
Else men are made their deodands.
Though they should wash their guilty hands
In this warm life-blood which doth part
From thine, and wound me to the heart,
Yet could they not be clean; their stain
Is dyed in such a purple grain.
There is not such another in
The world, to offer for their sin.
    Unconstant SYLVIO, when yet
I had not found him counterfeit,
One morning (I remember well),
Tied in this silver chain and bell,
Gave it to me: nay, and I know
What he said then, I'm sure I do:
Said he, 'Look how your huntsman here
Hath taught a fawn to hunt his deer.'
But SYLVIO soon had me beguiled;
This waxèd tame, while he grew wild,
And quite regardless of my smart,

Left me his fawn, but took his heart.
   Thenceforth I set myself to play
My solitary time away
With this; and, very well content,
Could so mine idle life have spent;
For it was full of sport, and light
Of foot and heart, and did invite
Me to its game: it seemed to bless
Itself in me; how could I less
Than love it? O, I cannot be
Unkind to a beast that loveth me.

   Had it lived long, I do not know
Whether it too might have done so
As SYLVIO did; his gifts might be
Perhaps as false, or more, than he;
But I am sure, for aught that I
Could in so short a time espy,
Thy love was far more better then
The love of false and cruel men.

   With sweetest milk and sugar first
I it at my own fingers nursed;
And as it grew, so every day
It waxed more white and sweet than they.
It had so sweet a breath! And oft
I blushed to see its foot more soft
And white, shall I say than my hand?
Nay, any lady's of the land.

   It is a wondrous thing how fleet
'Twas on those little silver feet;
With what a pretty skipping grace
It oft would challenge me the race;
And, when't had left me far away,
'Twould stay, and run again, and stay;
For it was nimbler much than hinds,
And trod as if on the four winds.

   I have a garden of my own,
But so with roses overgrown,
And lilies, that you would it guess
To be a little wilderness;
And all the spring-time of the year

It only lovèd to be there.
Among the beds of lilies I
Have sought it oft, where it should lie,
Yet could not, till itself would rise,
Find it, although before mine eyes;
For, in the flaxen lilies' shade,
It like a bank of lilies laid.
Upon the roses it would feed,
Until its lips e'en seem to bleed
And then to me 'twould boldly trip,
And print those roses on my lip.
But all its chief delight was still
On roses thus itself to fill,
And its pure virgin limbs to fold
In whitest sheets of lilies cold:
Had it lived long, it would have been
Lilies without, roses within.

   O help! O help! I see it faint
And die as calmly as a saint!
See how it weeps! the tears do come
Sad, slowly, dropping like a gum.
So weeps the wounded balsam; so
The holy frankincense doth flow;
The brotherless Heliades
Melt in such amber tears as these.

   I in a golden vial will
Keep these two crystal tears, and fill
It till it do o'erflow with mine,
Then place it in DIANA'S shrine.

   Now my sweet fawn is vanished to
Whither the swans and turtles go;
In fair Elysium to endure,
With milk-like lambs, and ermines pure.
O do not run too fast: for I
Will but bespeak thy grave, and die.

   First, my unhappy statue shall
Be cut in marble; and withal,
Let it be weeping too; but there
The engraver sure his art may spare;
For I so truly thee bemoan,

That I shall weep, though I be stone,
Until my tears, still dropping, wear
My breast, themselves engraving there;
There at my feet shalt thou be laid,
Of purest alabaster made;
For I would have thine image be
White as I can, though not as thee.

Young Love

I

Come, little infant, love me now,
   While thine unsuspected years
Clear thine agèd father's brow
   From cold jealousy and fears.

II

Pretty surely 'twere to see
   By young Love old Time beguiled,
While our sportings are as free
   As the nurse's with the child.

III

Common beauties stay fifteen;
   Such as yours should swifter move,
Whose fair blossoms are too green
   Yet for lust, but not for love.

IV

Love as much the snowy lamb,
   Or the wanton kid, does prize,
As the lusty bull or ram,
   For his morning sacrifice.

V

Now then love me: Time may take
  Thee before thy time away;
Of this need we'll virtue make,
  And learn love before we may.

VI

So we win of doubtful Fate,
  And, if good she to us meant,
We that good shall antedate,
  Or, if ill, that ill prevent.

VII

Thus as kingdoms, frustrating
  Other titles to their crown,
In the cradle crown their king,
  So all foreign claims to drown;

VIII

So to make all rivals vain,
  Now I crown thee with my love:
Crown me with thy love again,
  And we both shall monarchs prove.

To His Coy Mistress

Had we but world enough, and time,
This coyness, lady, were no crime.
We would sit down, and think which way
To walk, and pass our long love's day.
Thou by the Indian Ganges' side
Shouldst rubies find: I by the tide
Of Humber would complain. I would
Love you ten years before the flood,
And you should, if you please, refuse

Till the conversion of the Jews;
My vegetable love should grow
Vaster than empires and more slow;
An hundred years should go to praise
Thine eyes, and on thy forehead gaze;
Two hundred to adore each breast,
But thirty thousand to the rest;
An age at least to every part,
And the last age should show your heart.
For, lady, you deserve this state,
Nor would I love at lower rate.

    But at my back I always hear
Time's wingèd chariot hurrying near,
And yonder all before us lie
Deserts of vast eternity.
Thy beauty shall no more be found,
Nor, in thy marble vault, shall sound
My echoing song; then worms shall try
That long-preserved virginity,
And your quaint honour turn to dust,
And into ashes all my lust:
The grave's a fine and private place,
But none, I think, do there embrace.

    Now therefore, while the youthful hue
Sits on thy skin like morning dew,
And while thy willing soul transpires
At every pore with instant fires,
Now let us sport us while we may,
And now, like amorous birds of prey,
Rather at once our time devour,
Than languish in his slow-chapt power.
Let us roll all our strength and all
Our sweetness up into one ball,
And tear our pleasures with rough strife,
Thorough the iron gates of life;
Thus, though we cannot make our sun
Stand still, yet we will make him run.

The Unfortunate Lover

Alas! how pleasant are their days,
With whom the infant love yet plays!
Sorted by pairs, they still are seen
By fountains cool and shadows green;
But soon these flames do lose their light,
Like meteors of a summer's night;
Nor can they to that region climb,
To make impression upon Time.

   'Twas in a shipwreck, when the seas
Ruled, and the winds did what they please,
That my poor lover floating lay,
And, ere brought forth, was cast away;
Till at the last the master wave
Upon the rock his mother drave,
And there she split against the stone,
In a Cæsarian section.

The sea him lent these bitter tears,
Which at his eyes he always bears,
And from the winds the sighs he bore,
Which through his surging breast do roar;
No day he saw but that which breaks
Through frighted clouds in forkèd streaks,
While round the rattling thunder hurled,
As at the funeral of the world.

While Nature to his birth presents
This masque of quarrelling elements,
A numerous fleet of cormorants black,
That sailed insulting o'er the wrack,
Received into their cruel care
The unfortunate and abject heir;
Guardians most fit to entertain
The orphan of the hurricane.

They fed him up with hopes and air,
Which soon digested to despair,
And as one cormorant fed him, still
Another on his heart did bill;
Thus, while they famish him and feast,
He both consumèd, and increased,
And languishèd with doubtful breath,
The amphibium of life and death.

And now, when angry Heaven would
Behold a spectacle of blood,
Fortune and he are called to play
At sharp before it all the day,
And tyrant Love his breast does ply
With all his winged artillery,
Whilst he, betwixt the flames and waves,
Like Ajax, the mad tempest braves.

See how he nak'd and fierce does stand,
Cuffing the thunder with one hand,
While with the other he does lock,
And grapple, with the stubborn rock,
From which he with each wave rebounds,
Torn into flames, and ragg'd with wounds;
And all he says, a lover drest
In his own blood does relish best.

This is the only banneret
That ever Love created yet;
Who, though by the malignant stars,
Forcèd to live in storms and wars,
Yet dying, leaves a perfume here,
And music within every ear;
And he in story only rules,
In a field sable, a lover gules.

The Gallery

Chlora, come view my soul, and tell
Whether I have contrived it well:
Now all its several lodgings lie,
Composed into one gallery,
And the great arras-hangings, made
Of various facings, by are laid,
That, for all furniture, you'll find
Only your picture in my mind.

Here thou art painted in the dress
Of an inhuman murderess;
Examining upon our hearts,
(Thy fertile shop of cruel arts,)
Engines more keen than ever yet
Adornèd tyrant's cabinet,
Of which the most tormenting are,
Black eyes, red lips, and curlèd hair.

But, on the other side, thou'rt drawn,
Like to AURORA in the dawn;
When in the east she slumbering lies,
And stretches out her milky thighs,
While all the morning quire does sing,
And manna falls and roses spring,
And, at thy feet, the wooing doves
Sit perfecting their harmless loves.

Like an enchantress here thou show'st,
Vexing thy restless lover's ghost;
And, by a light obscure, dost rave
Over his entrails, in the cave,
Divining thence, with horrid care,
How long thou shalt continue fair;
And (when informed) them throw'st away
To be the greedy vulture's prey.

But, against that, thou sitt'st afloat,
Like VENUS in her pearly boat;
The halcyons, calming all that's nigh,
Betwixt the air and water fly;
Or, if some rolling wave appears,
A mass of ambergris it bears,
Nor blows more wind than what may well
Convoy the perfume to the smell.

These pictures, and a thousand more,
Of thee, my gallery doth store,
In all the forms thou canst invent,
Either to please me, or torment;
For thou alone, to people me,
Art grown a numerous colony,
And a collection choicer far
Than or Whitehall's, or Mantua's were.

But of these pictures, and the rest,
That at the entrance likes me best,
Where the same posture and the look
Remains with which I first was took;
A tender shepherdess, whose hair
Hangs loosely playing in the air,
Transplanting flowers from the green hill
To crown her head and bosom fill.

The Fair Singer

I

To make a final conquest of all me,
Love did compose so sweet an enemy,
In whom both beauties to my death agree,
Joining themselves in fatal harmony,
That, while she with her eyes my heart does bind,
She with her voice might captivate my mind.

II

I could have fled from one but singly fair;
My disentangled soul itself might save,
Breaking the curlèd trammels of her hair;
But how should I avoid to be her slave,
Whose subtle art invisibly can wreathe
My fetters of the very air I breathe?

III

It had been easy fighting in some plain,
Where victory might hang in equal choice,
But all resistance against her is vain,
Who has the advantage both of eyes and voice;
And all my forces needs must be undone,
She having gainèd both the wind and sun.

Mourning

I

You, that decipher out the fate
  Of human offsprings from the skies,
What mean these infants which, of late,
  Spring from the stars of Chlora's eyes?

II

Her eyes confused, and doubled o'er
  With tears suspended ere they flow,
Seem bending upwards to restore
  To Heaven, whence it came, their woe.

III

When, moulding of the watery spheres,
  Slow drops untie themselves away,
As if she with those precious tears
  Would strew the ground where Strephon lay.

IV

Yet some affirm, pretending art,
  Her eyes have so her bosom drowned,
Only to soften, near her heart,
  A place to fix another wound.

V

And, while vain pomp does her restrain
  Within her solitary bower,
She courts herself in amorous rain,
  Herself both Danae and the shower.

VI

Nay others, bolder, hence esteem
  Joy now so much her master grown,
That whatsoever does but seem
  Like grief is from her windows thrown.

VII

Nor that she pays, while she survives,
    To her dead love this tribute due,
But casts abroad these donatives,
    At the installing of a new.

VIII

How wide they dream! the Indian slaves,
    That sink for pearl through seas profound,
Would find her tears yet deeper waves,
    And not of one the bottom sound.

IX

I yet my silent judgment keep,
    Disputing not what they believe:
But sure as oft as women weep,
    It is to be supposed they grieve.

Daphnis and Chloe

I

Daphnis must from Chloe part;
   Now is come the dismal hour,
   That must all his hopes devour,
All his labour, all his art.

II

Nature, her own sex's foe,
   Long had taught her to be coy;
   But she neither knew to enjoy,
Nor yet let her lover go.

III

But, with this sad news, surprised,
   Soon she let that niceness fall,
   And would gladly yield to all,
So it had his stay comprised.

IV

Nature so herself does use
   To lay by her wonted state,
   Lest the world should separate;
Sudden parting closer glues.

V

He, well read in all the ways
   By which men their siege maintain,
   Knew not that, the fort to gain,
Better 'twas the siege to raise.

VI

But he came so full possessed
   With the grief of parting thence,
   That he had not so much sense
As to see he might be blessed;

VII

Till love, in her language, breathed
  Words she never spake before;
  But than legacies no more,
To a dying man bequeathed.

VIII

For alas! the time was spent;
  Now the latest minute's run,
  When poor Daphnis is undone,
Between joy and sorrow rent.

IX

At that 'Why?' that 'Stay, my dear!'
  His disordered locks he tare,
  And with rolling eyes did glare,
And his cruel fate forswear.

X

As the soul of one scarce dead,
  With the shrieks of friends aghast,
  Looks distracted back in haste,
And then straight again is fled;

XI

So did wretched Daphnis look,
  Frighting her he lovèd most;
  At the last this lover's ghost
Thus his leave resolvèd took.

XII

'Are my hell and heaven joined,
  More to torture him that dies?
  Could departure not suffice,
But that you must then grow kind?

XIII

'Ah! my Chloe, how have I
  Such a wretched minute found,
  When thy favours should me wound,
More than all thy cruelty?

XIV

'So to the condemnèd wight
   The delicious cup we fill,
   And allow him all he will,
For his last and short delight.

XV

'But I will not now begin
   Such a debt unto my foe,
   Nor to my departure owe,
What my presence could not win.

XVI

'Absence is too much alone;
   Better 'tis to go in peace,
   Than my losses to increase,
By a late fruition.

XVII

'Why should I enrich my fate?
   'Tis a vanity to wear,
   For my executioner,
Jewels of so high a rate.

XVIII

'Rather I away will pine,
   In a manly stubbornness,
   Then be fatted up express
For the cannibal to dine.

XIX

'Whilst this grief does thee disarm,
   All the enjoyment of our love
   But the ravishment would prove
Of a body dead while warm;

XX

'And I parting should appear
   Like the gourmand Hebrew dead,
   While, with quails and manna fed,
He does through the desert err;

XXI

'Or the witch that midnight wakes
For the fern, whose magic weed
In one minute cast the seed
And invisible him makes.

XXII

'Gentler times for love are meant:
Who for parting pleasure strain,
Gather roses in the rain,
Wet themselves and spoil their scent.

XXIII

'Farewell, therefore, all the fruit
Which I could from love receive:
Joy will not with sorrow weave,
Nor will I this grief pollute.

XXIV

'Fate, I come, as dark, as sad,
As thy malice could desire;
Yet bring with me all the fire
That Love in his torches had.'

XXV

At these words away he broke,
As who long has praying lien,
To his head's-man makes the sign
And receives the parting stroke.

XXVI

But hence, virgins all, beware;
Last night he with Phlogis slept,
This night for Dorinda kept,
And but rid to take the air.

XXVII

Yet he does himself excuse;
Nor indeed without a cause:
For, according to the laws,
Why did Chloe once refuse?

The Definition of Love

I

My Love is of a birth as rare
   As 'tis, for object, strange and high;
It was begotten by Despair,
   Upon Impossibility.

II

Magnanimous Despair alone
   Could show me so divine a thing,
Where feeble hope could ne'er have flown,
   But vainly flapped its tinsel wing.

III

And yet I quickly might arrive
   Where my extended soul is fixed;
But Fate does iron wedges drive,
   And always crowds itself betwixt.

IV

For Fate with jealous eye does see
   Two perfect loves, nor lets them close;
Their union would her ruin be,
   And her tyrannic power depose

V

And therefore her decrees of steel
   Us as the distant poles have placed,
(Though Love's whole world on us doth wheel),
   Not by themselves to be embraced,

VI

Unless the giddy heaven fall,
   And earth some new convulsion tear,
And, us to join, the world should all
   Be cramped into a planisphere.

VII

As lines, so love's oblique, may well
   Themselves in every angle greet:
But ours, so truly parallel,
   Though infinite, can never meet.

VIII

Therefore the love which us doth bind,
   But Fate so enviously debars,
Is the conjunction of the mind,
   And opposition of the stars.

The Picture of Little T. C.
in a Prospect of Flowers

I

See with what simplicity
This nymph begins her golden days!
In the green grass she loves to lie,
And there with her fair aspect tames
The wilder flowers and gives them names,
But only with the roses plays,
          And them does tell
What colour best becomes them and what smell.

II

Who can foretell for what high cause
This darling of the Gods was born?
Yet this is she whose chaster laws
The wanton Love shall one day fear,
And, under her command severe,
See his bow broke, and ensigns torn.
          Happy who can
Appease this virtuous enemy of man!

III

O then let me in time compound
And parley with those conquering eyes,
Ere they have tried their force to wound;
Ere with their glancing wheels they drive
In triumph over hearts that strive,
And them that yield but more despise:
          Let me be laid
Where I may see the glories from some shade.

IV

Meantime, whilst every verdant thing
Itself does at thy beauty charm,
Reform the errors of the spring;
Make that the tulips may have share
Of sweetness, seeing they are fair;
And roses of their thorns disarm;
    But most procure
That violets may a longer age endure.

V

But O, young beauty of the woods,
Whom Nature courts with fruit and flowers,
Gather the flowers, but spare the buds,
Lest FLORA, angry at thy crime
To kill her infants in their prime,
Do quickly make the example yours;
    And ere we see,
Nip in the blossom, all our hopes and thee.

A Dialogue between Thyrsis and Dorinda

Dorinda	When death shall snatch us from these kids,
	And shut up our divided lids,
	Tell me, Thyrsis, prythee do,
	Whither thou and I must go?
Thyrsis	To the Elysium.
Dorinda	Oh, where is't?
Thyrsis	A chaste soul can never miss't.
Dorinda	I know no way but one; our home
	Is our Elysium.
Thyrsis	Cast thine eye to yonder sky,
	There the milky way doth lie;
	'Tis a sure, but rugged way,
	That leads to everlasting day.
Dorinda	There birds may nest, but how can I,
	That have no wings and cannot fly?
Thyrsis	Do not sigh, fair nymph, for fire
	Hath no wings, yet doth aspire
	Till it hit against the pole;
	Heaven's the centre of the soul.
Dorinda	But in Elysium how do they
	Pass eternity away?
Thyrsis	O! there's neither hope nor fear,
	There's no wolf, no fox, no bear,
	No need of dog to fetch our stray,
	Our Lightfoot we may give away;
	And there, most sweetly, may thine ear
	Feast with the music of the sphere.
Dorinda	How I my future state,
	By silent thinking, antedate!
	I prythee let us spend our time to come,
	In talking of Elysium.

Thyrsis   Then I'll go on: there sheep are full
Of softest grass, and softest wool;
There birds sing concerts, garlands grow,
Cool winds do whisper, springs do flow;
There always is a rising sun,
And day is ever but begun;
Shepherds there bear equal sway,
And every nymph's a queen of May.

Dorinda   Ah me! ah me!

Thyrsis   DORINDA, why dost cry?

Dorinda   I'm sick, I'm sick, and fain would die.

Thyrsis   Convince me now that this is true
By bidding, with me, all adieu.

Dorinda   I cannot live without thee, I
Will for thee, much more with thee, die.

Thyrsis   Then let us give CORELLIA charge o' the sheep.
And thou and I'll pick poppies and them steep
In wine, and drink on't even till we weep,
So shall we smoothly pass away in sleep.

The Match

I

Nature had long a treasure made
   Of all her choicest store,
Fearing, when she should be decayed,
   To beg in vain for more.

II

Her orientest colours there,
   And essences most pure,
With sweetest perfumes hoarded were,
   All, as she thought, secure.

III

She seldom them unlocked or used
   But with the nicest care;
For, with one grain of them diffused,
   She could the world repair.

IV

But likeness soon together drew,
   What she did separate lay;
Of which one perfect beauty grew,
   And that was CELIA.

V

Love wisely had of long foreseen
   That he must once grow old,
And therefore stored a magazine
   To save him from the cold.

VI

He kept the several cells replete
   With nitre thrice refined,
The naphtha's and the sulphur's heat,
   And all that burns the mind.

VII

He fortified the double gate,
    And rarely thither came;
For, with one spark of these, he straight
    All Nature could inflame.

VIII

Till, by vicinity so long,
    A nearer way they sought,
And, grown magnetically strong,
    Into each other wrought.

IX

Thus all his fuel did unite
    To make one fire high:
None ever burned so hot, so bright;
    And, CELIA, that am I.

X

So we alone the happy, rest,
    Whilst all the world is poor,
And have within ourselves possessed
    All Love's and Nature's store.

The Mower, against Gardens

Luxurious man, to bring his vice in use,
    Did after him the world seduce,
And from the fields the flowers and plants allure,
    Where Nature was most plain and pure.
He first inclosed within the gardens square
    A dead and standing pool of air,
And a more luscious earth for them did knead,
    Which stupefied them while it fed.
The pink grew then as double as his mind;
    The nutriment did change the kind.
With strange perfumes he did the roses taint;
    And flowers themselves were taught to paint.
The tulip white did for complexion seek,
    And learned to interline its cheek;
Its onion root they then so high did hold,
    That one was for a meadow sold:
Another world was searched through oceans new,
    To find the marvel of Peru;
And yet these rarities might be allowed
    To man, that sovereign thing and proud,
Had he not dealt between the bark and tree,
    Forbidden mixtures there to see.
No plant now knew the stock from which it came;
    He grafts upon the wild the tame,
That the uncertain and adulterate fruit
    Might put the palate in dispute.
His green seraglio has its eunuchs too,
    Lest any tyrant him outdo;
And in the cherry he does Nature vex,
    To procreate without a sex.
'Tis all enforced, the fountain and the grot,
    While the sweet fields do lie forgot,
Where willing Nature does to all dispense
    A wild and fragrant innocence;
And fauns and fairies do the meadows till
    More by their presence than their skill.
Their statues polished by some ancient hand,

May to adorn the gardens stand;
But, howsoe'er the figures do excel,
   The Gods themselves with us do dwell.

Damon the Mower

Hark how the mower DAMON sung,
With love of JULIANA stung!
While everything did seem to paint
The scene more fit for his complaint.
Like her fair eyes the day was fair,
But scorching like his amorous care;
Sharp, like his scythe, his sorrow was,
And withered, like his hopes, the grass.

   Oh what unusual heats are here,
Which thus our sun-burned meadows fear!
The grasshopper its pipe gives o'er,
And hamstringed frogs can dance no more;
But in the brook the green frog wades,
And grasshoppers seek out the shades;
Only the snake, that kept within,
Now glitters in its second skin.

   This heat the sun could never raise,
Nor dog-star so inflame the days;
It from an higher beauty grow'th,
Which burns the fields and mower both;
Which made the dog, and makes the sun
Hotter than his own Phaeton;
Not July causeth these extremes,
But JULIANA'S scorching beams.

   Tell me where I may pass the fires
Of the hot day, or hot desires;
To what cool cave shall I descend,
Or to what gelid fountain bend?

Alas! I look for ease in vain,
When remedies themselves complain;
No moisture but my tears do rest,
No cold but in her icy breast.

How long wilt thou, fair shepherdess,
Esteem me and my presents less?
To thee the harmless snake I bring,
Disarmèd of its teeth and sting;
To thee chameleons, changing hue,
And oak leaves tipt with honey dew;
Yet thou ungrateful hast not sought
Nor what they are, nor who them brought.

I am the mower DAMON, known
Through all the meadows I have mown.
On me the morn her dew distils
Before her darling daffodils;
And, if at noon my toil me heat,
The sun himself licks off my sweat;
While, going home, the evening sweet
In cowslip-water bathes my feet.

What though the piping shepherd stock
The plains with an unnumbered flock,
This scythe of mine discovers wide
More ground than all his sheep do hide.
With this the golden fleece I shear
Of all these closes every year,
And though in wool more pure than they,
Yet I am richer far in hay.

Nor am I so deformed to sight,
If in my scythe I lookèd right;
In which I see my picture done,
As in a crescent moon the sun.
The deathless fairies take me oft
To lead them in their dances soft;
And when I tune myself to sing,
About me they contract their ring.

How happy might I still have mowed,
Had not Love here his thistle sowed!
But now I all the day complain,
Joining my labour to my pain;
And with my scythe cut down the grass,
Yet still my grief is where it was;
But, when the iron blunter grows,
Sighing I whet my scythe and woes.

While thus he drew his elbow round,
Depopulating all the ground,
And, with his whistling scythe, does cut
Each stroke between the earth and root,
The edgèd steel, by careless chance,
Did into his own ankle glance,
And there among the grass fell down
By his own scythe the mower mown.

Alas! said he, these hurts are slight
To those that die by Love's despite.
With shepherd's purse, and clown's all-heal,
The blood I stanch and wound I seal.
Only for him no cure is found,
Whom JULIANA'S eyes do wound;
'Tis Death alone that this must do;
For, Death, thou art a Mower too.

The Mower to the Glow-worms

I

Ye living lamps, by whose dear light
The nightingale does sit so late,
And studying all the summer night,
Her matchless songs does meditate;

II

Ye country comets, that portend
No war nor prince's funeral,
Shining unto no higher end
Than to presage the grass's fall;

III

Ye glow-worms, whose officious flame
To wandering mowers shows the way,
That in the night have lost their aim,
And after foolish fires do stray;

IV

Your courteous lights in vain you waste,
Since JULIANA here is come,
For she my mind hath so displaced,
That I shall never find my home.

The Mower's Song

I

My mind was once the true survey
Of all these meadows fresh and gay,
And in the greenness of the grass
Did see its hopes as in a glass;
When JULIANA came, and she,
What I do to the grass, does to my thoughts and me.

II

But these, while I with sorrow pine,
Grew more luxuriant still and fine,
That not one blade of grass you spied,
But had a flower on either side;
When JULIANA came, and she,
What I do to the grass, does to my thoughts and me.

III

Unthankful meadows, could you so
A fellowship so true forego,
And in your gaudy May-games meet,
While I lay trodden under feet?
When JULIANA came, and she,
What I do to the grass, does to my thoughts and me?

IV

But what you in compassion ought,
Shall now by my revenge be wrought;
And flowers, and grass, and I, and all,
Will in one common ruin fall;
For JULIANA comes, and she,
What I do to the grass, does to my thoughts and me.

V

And thus, ye meadows, which have been
Companions of my thoughts more green,
Shall now the heraldry become
With which I shall adorn my tomb;
For JULIANA came, and she,
What I do to the grass, does to my thoughts and me.

Ametas and Thestylis Making Hay-ropes

Ametas   Think'st thou that this love can stand,
         Whilst thou still dost say me nay?
     Love unpaid does soon disband:
         Love binds love, as hay binds hay.

Thestylis   Think'st thou that this rope would twine,
         If we both should turn one way?
     Where both parties so combine,
         Neither love will twist, nor hay.

Ametas   Thus you vain excuses find,
         Which yourself and us delay:
     And love ties a woman's mind
         Looser than with ropes of hay.

Thestylis   What you cannot constant hope
         Must be taken as you may.

Ametas   Then let's both lay by our rope,
         And go kiss within the hay.

Music's Empire

First was the world as one great cymbal made,
Where jarring winds to infant nature played;
All music was a solitary sound,
To hollow rocks and murmuring fountains bound.

Jubal first made the wilder notes agree,
And Jubal tunèd Music's Jubilee;
He called the echoes from their sullen cell,
And built the organ's city, where they dwell.

Each sought a consort in that lovely place,
And virgin trebles wed the manly bass,
From whence the progeny of numbers new
Into harmonious colonies withdrew;

Some to the lute, some to the viol went,
And others chose the cornet eloquent;
These practising the wind, and those the wire,
To sing man's triumphs, or in Heaven's choir.

Then music, the mosaic of the air,
Did of all these a solemn noise prepare,
With which she gained the empire of the ear,
Including all between the earth and sphere.

Victorious sounds! yet here your homage do
Unto a gentler conqueror than you;
Who, though he flies the music of his praise,
Would with you Heaven's hallelujahs raise.

Translated from Seneca's
Tragedy of Thyestes

CHORUS II

Stet quicunque volet potens
Aulae culmine lubrico, &c.

Climb, at Court, for me, that will,
Tottering favour's pinnacle;
All I seek is to lie still:
Settled in some secret nest,
In calm leisure let me rest,
And, far off the public stage,
Pass away my silent age.
Thus, when, without noise, unknown,
I have lived out all my span,
I shall die, without a groan,
An old honest countryman.
Who, exposed to others' eyes,
Into his own heart ne'er pries,
Death to him's a strange surprise.

On a Drop of Dew

See, how the orient dew,
Shed from the bosom of the morn
    Into the blowing roses,
    (Yet careless of its mansion new,
For the clear region where 'twas born,)
    Round in itself incloses;
    And, in its little globe's extent,
Frames, as it can, its native element.
    How it the purple flower does slight,

Scarce touching where it lies;
But gazing back upon the skies,
Shines with a mournful light,
Like its own tear,
Because so long divided from the sphere.
Restless it rolls, and unsecure,
Trembling, lest it grow impure;
Till the warm sun pity its pain,
And to the skies exhale it back again.
So the soul, that drop, that ray
Of the clear fountain of eternal day,
(Could it within the human flower be seen,)
Remembering still its former height,
Shuns the sweet leaves, and blossoms green,
And, recollecting its own light,
Does, in its pure and circling thoughts, express
The greater heaven in an heaven less.
In how coy a figure wound,
Every way it turns away;
So the world-excluding round,
Yet receiving in the day;
Dark beneath, but bright above,
Here disdaining, there in love.
How loose and easy hence to go;
How girt and ready to ascend;
Moving but on a point below,
It all about does upwards bend.
Such did the manna's sacred dew distil;
White and entire, though congealed and chill;
Congealed on earth; but does, dissolving, run
Into the glories of the almighty sun.

The Garden

How vainly men themselves amaze,
To win the palm, the oak, or bays;
And their incessant labours see
Crowned from some single herb, or tree,
Whose short and narrow-vergèd shade
Does prudently their toils upbraid;
While all the flowers and trees do close,
To weave the garlands of repose!

Fair Quiet, have I found thee here,
And Innocence, thy sister dear?
Mistaken long, I sought you then
In busy companies of men.
Your sacred plants, if here below,
Only among the plants will grow;
Society is all but rude
To this delicious solitude.

No white nor red was ever seen
So amorous as this lovely green.
Fond lovers, cruel as their flame,
Cut in these trees their mistress' name:
Little, alas! they know or heed,
How far these beauties hers exceed!
Fair trees! wheres'e'er your bark I wound,
No name shall but your own be found.

When we have run our passion's heat,
Love hither makes his best retreat.
The gods, that mortal beauty chase,
Still in a tree did end their race;
Apollo hunted Daphne so,
Only that she might laurel grow;
And Pan did after Syrinx speed,
Not as a nymph, but for a reed.

What wondrous life is this I lead!
Ripe apples drop about my head;
The luscious clusters of the vine

Upon my mouth do crush their wine;
The nectarine, and curious peach,
Into my hands themselves do reach;
Stumbling on melons, as I pass,
Insnared with flowers, I fall on grass.

Meanwhile the mind, from pleasure less,
Withdraws into its happiness;
The mind, that ocean where each kind
Does straight its own resemblance find;
Yet it creates, transcending these,
Far other worlds, and other seas,
Annihilating all that's made
To a green thought in a green shade.

Here at the fountain's sliding foot,
Or at some fruit-tree's mossy root,
Casting the body's vest aside,
My soul into the boughs does glide:
There, like a bird, it sits and sings,
Then whets and combs its silver wings,
And, till prepared for longer flight,
Waves in its plumes the various light.

Such was that happy garden-state,
While man there walked without a mate:
After a place so pure and sweet,
What other help could yet be meet!
But 'twas beyond a mortal's share
To wander solitary there:
Two paradises 'twere in one,
To live in paradise alone.

How well the skilful gardener drew
Of flowers, and herbs, this dial new;
Where, from above, the milder sun
Does through a fragrant zodiac run,
And, as it works, the industrious bee
Computes its time as well as we!
How could such sweet and wholesome hours
Be reckoned but with herbs and flowers?

Upon the Death of the Lord Hastings

Go, intercept some fountain in the vein,
Whose virgin-source yet never steeped the plain.
Hastings is dead, and we must find a store
Of tears untouched, and never wept before.
Go, stand betwixt the morning and the flowers;
And, ere they fall, arrest the early showers.
Hastings is dead; and we, disconsolate,
With early tears must mourn his early fate.

Alas! his virtues did his death presage:
Needs must he die, that doth outrun his age;
The phlegmatic and slow prolongs his day,
And on Time's wheel sticks like a remora.
What man is he, that hath not Heaven beguiled,
And is not thence mistaken for a child?
While those of growth more sudden, and more bold,
Are hurried hence, as if already old;
For, there above, they number not as here,
But weigh to man the Geometric Year.

Had he but at this measure still increased,
And on the Tree of Life once made a feast,
As that of knowledge, what loves had he given
To earth, and then what jealousies to Heaven!
But 'tis a maxim of that state, that none,
Lest he become like them, taste more than one.
Therefore the democratic stars did rise,
And all that worth from hence did ostracize.

Yet as some prince, that, for state jealousy,
Secures his nearest and most loved ally,
His thought with richest triumphs entertains,
And in the choicest pleasure charms his pains;
So he, not banished hence, but there confined,
There better recreates his active mind.

Before the crystal palace where he dwells
The armèd angels hold their carousals;
And underneath he views the tournaments
Of all these sublunary elements.
But most he doth the Eternal Book behold,

On which the happy names do stand enrolled;
And gladly there can all his kindred claim,
But most rejoices at his mother's name.
   The Gods themselves cannot their joy conceal,
But draw their veils, and their pure beams reveal:
Only they drooping Hymeneus note,
Who for sad purple tears his saffron-coat,
And trails his torches through the starry hall,
Reversèd at his darling's funeral.
   And Æsculapius, who, ashamed and stern,
Himself at once condemneth and Mayerne;
Like some sad chemist, who, prepared to reap
The golden harvest, sees his glasses leap.
For, how immortal must their race have stood,
Had Mayerne once been mixed with Hastings' blood!
How sweet and verdant would these laurels be,
Had they been planted on that balsam tree!
But what could he, good man, although he bruised
All herbs, and them a thousand ways infused?
All he had tried, but all in vain, he saw,
And wept, as we, without redress or law.
For man, alas! is but the Heaven's sport;
And Art indeed is long, but Life is short.

To His Noble Friend,
Mr Richard Lovelace,
upon His Poems

SIR,

Our times are much degenerate from those
Which your sweet muse, which your good fortune chose;
And as complexions alter with the climes,
Our wits have drawn the infection of our times,
That candid Age no other way could tell
To be ingenious, but by speaking well.
Who best could praise had then the greatest praise;
'Twas more esteemed to give than wear the bays.
Modest Ambition studied only then
To honour, not herself, but worthy men.
These virtues now are banished out of town,
Our civil wars have lost the civic crown.
He highest builds who with most art destroys,
And against others' fame his own employs.
I see the envious caterpillar sit
On the fair blossom of each growing wit.
    The air's already tainted with the swarms
Of insects, which against you rise in arms.
Word-peckers, paper-rats, book-scorpions,
Of wit corrupted, the unfashioned sons.
The barbèd censurers begin to look
Like the grim Consistory on thy book;
And on each line cast a reforming eye,
Severer than the young Presbytery.
Till when in vain they have thee all perused,
You shall for being faultless be accused.
Some reading your *Lucasta* will allege
You wronged in her the Houses' privilege;
Some that you under sequestration are,
Because you write when going to the war;
And one the book prohibits, because Kent
Their first petition by the author sent.
    But when the beauteous ladies came to know

That their dear Lovelace was endangered so;
Lovelace, that thawed the most congealed breast,
He who loved best, and them defended best,
Whose hand so rudely grasps the steely brand,
Whose hand so gently melts the lady's hand;
They all in mutiny, though yet undressed,
Sallied, and would in his defence contest.
And one, the loveliest that was yet ere seen,
Thinking that I too of the rout had been,
Mine eyes invaded with a female spite
(She knew what pain 'twould be to lose that sight).
O no, mistake not, I replied: for I
In your defence, or in his cause, would die;
But he, secure of glory and of time,
Above their envy or mine aid doth climb.
Him valiant'st men and fairest nymphs approve,
His book in them finds judgment, with you, love.

To His Worthy Friend, Doctor Witty,

UPON HIS TRANSLATION OF
THE 'POPULAR ERRORS.'

Sit farther and make room for thine own fame,
Where just desert enrols thy honoured name,
The Good Interpreter. Some in this task
Take off the cypress veil, but leave a mask,
Changing the Latin, but do more obscure
That sense in English which was bright and pure.
So of translators they are authors grown,
For ill translators make the book their own.
Others do strive with words and forcèd phrase
To add such lustre, and so many rays,
That but to make the vessel shining, they
Much of the precious metal rub away.
He is translation's thief that addeth more,
As much as he that taketh from the store

Of the first author. Here he maketh blots,
That mends; and added beauties are but spots.
   CÆLIA, whose English doth more richly flow
Than Tagus, purer than dissolvèd snow,
And sweet as are her lips that speak it, she
Now learns the tongues of France and Italy;
But she is CÆLIA still; no other grace
But her own smiles commend that lovely face;
Her native beauty's not Italianated,
Nor her chaste mind into the French translated;
Her thoughts are English, though her speaking wit
With other language doth them fitly fit.
   Translators, learn of her: but stay, I slide
Down into error with the vulgar tide;
Women must not teach here: the doctor doth
Stint them to cordials, almond-milk, and broth.
Now I reform, and surely as will all
Whose happy eyes on thy translation fall.
I see the people hastening to thy book,
Liking themselves the worse the more they look,
And so disliking, that they nothing see
Now worth the liking, but thy book and thee.
And (if I judgment have) I censure right,
For something guides my hand that I must write;
You have translation's statutes best fulfilled,
That handling neither sully nor would gild.

On Paradise Lost

When I beheld the poet blind, yet bold,
In slender book his vast design unfold,
Messiah crowned, God's reconciled decree,
Rebelling angels, the forbidden tree,
Heaven, hell, earth, chaos, all; the argument
Held me awhile misdoubting his intent,
That he would ruin (for I saw him strong)

The sacred truths to fable and old song,
(So Samson groped the temple's posts in spite)
The world o'erwhelming to revenge his sight.

    Yet as I read, soon growing less severe,
I liked his project, the success did fear;
Through that wide field how he his way should find,
O'er which lame faith leads understanding blind;
Lest he perplexed the things he would explain,
And what was easy he should render vain.

    Or if a work so infinite he spanned,
Jealous I was that some less skilful hand
(Such as disquiet always what is well,
And by ill imitating would excel)
Might hence presume the whole creation's day
To change in scenes, and show it in a play.

    Pardon me, mighty poet, nor despise
My causeless, yet not impious, surmise.
But I am now convinced, and none will dare
Within thy labours to pretend a share.
Thou hast not missed one thought that could be fit,
And all that was improper dost omit;
So that no room is here for writers left,
But to detect their ignorance or theft.

    That majesty which through thy work doth reign
Draws the devout, deterring the profane;
And things divine thou treat'st of in such state
As them preserves, and thee, inviolate.
At once delight and horror on us seize,
Thou sing'st with so much gravity and ease,
And above human flight dost soar aloft,
With plume so strong, so equal, and so soft:
The bird named from that paradise you sing
So never flags, but always keeps on wing.
Where couldst thou words of such a compass find?
Whence furnish such a vast expanse of mind?
Just Heaven thee, like Tiresias, to requite,
Rewards with prophecy thy loss of sight.

    Well mightst thou scorn thy readers to allure
With tinkling rhyme, of thy own sense secure,
While the Town-Bayes writes all the while and spells,

And like a pack-horse tires without his bells.
Their fancies like our bushy points appear:
The poets tag them, we for fashion wear.
I too, transported by the mode, offend,
And while I meant to praise thee, mis-commend;
Thy verse created like thy theme sublime,
In number, weight, and measure, needs not rhyme.

An Epitaph upon —

Enough; and leave the rest to fame;
'Tis to commend her, but to name.
Courtship, which, living, she declined,
When dead, to offer were unkind.
Where never any could speak ill,
Who would officious praises spill?
Nor can the truest wit, or friend,
Without detracting, her commend;
To say, she lived a virgin chaste
In this age loose and all unlaced;
Nor was, when vice is so allowed,
Of virtue or ashamed or proud;
That her soul was on Heaven so bent,
No minute but it came and went;
That, ready her last debt to pay,
She summed her life up every day;
Modest as morn, as mid-day bright,
Gentle as evening, cool as night:
'Tis true; but all too weakly said;
'Twas more significant, she's dead.

Two Songs

AT THE MARRIAGE OF THE LORD FAUCONBERG
AND THE LADY MARY CROMWELL

FIRST SONG

Chorus, Endymion, Luna

Chorus	The astrologer's own eyes are set,
	And even wolves the sheep forget;
	Only this shepherd, late and soon,
	Upon this hill outwakes the moon;
	Hark how he sings with sad delight,
	Thorough the clear and silent night!
Endymion	CYNTHIA, O CYNTHIA, turn thine ear,
	Nor scorn ENDYMION'S plaints to hear!
	As we our flocks, so you command
	The fleecy clouds with silver wand.
Cynthia	If thou a mortal, rather sleep;
	Or if a shepherd, watch thy sheep.
Endymion	The shepherd, since he saw thine eyes,
	And sheep, are both thy sacrifice;
	Nor merits he a mortal's name,
	That burns with an immortal flame.
Cynthia	I have enough for me to do,
	Ruling the waves that ebb and flow.
Endymion	Since thou disdain'st not then to share
	On sublunary things thy care,
	Rather restrain these double seas,
	Mine eyes, incessant deluges.
Cynthia	My wakeful lamp all night must move,
	Securing their repose above.
Endymion	If therefore thy resplendent ray
	Can make a night more bright than day,
	Shine thorough this obscurer breast,
	With shades of deep despair oppressed.

Chorus	Courage, ENDYMION, boldly woo!
	ANCHISES was a shepherd too,
	Yet is her younger sister laid
	Sporting with him in IDA'S shade:
	· And CYNTHIA, though the strongest,
	Seeks but the honour to have held out
	longest.
Endymion	Here unto Latmos' top I climb,
	How far below thine orb sublime!
	O why, as well as eyes to see,
	Have I not arms that reach to thee?
Cynthia	'Tis needless then that I refuse,
	Would you but your own reason use.
Endymion	Though I so high may not pretend,
	It is the same, so you descend.
Cynthia	These stars would say I do them wrong,
	Rivals, each one, for thee too strong.
Endymion	The stars are fixed unto their sphere
	And cannot, though they would, come
	near.
	Less loves set off each other's praise,
	While stars eclipse by mixing rays.
Cynthia	That cave is dark.
Endymion	Then none can spy:
	Or shine thou there, and 'tis the sky.
Chorus	Joy to ENDYMION!
	For he has CYNTHIA'S favour won,
	And JOVE himself approves
	With his serenest influence their loves.
	For he did never love to pair
	His progeny above the air;
	But to be honest, valiant, wise,
	Makes mortals matches fit for deities.

SECOND SONG

Hobbinol, Phillis, Tomalin

Hobbinol PHILLIS, TOMALIN, away!
 Never such a merry day,
 For the northern shepherd's son
 Has MENALCAS' daughter won.

Phillis Stay till I some flowers have tied
 In a garland for the bride.

Tomalin If thou wouldst a garland bring,
 PHILLIS, you may wait the spring:
 They have chosen such an hour
 When she is the only flower.

Phillis Let's not then, at least, be seen
 Without each a sprig of green.

Hobbinol Fear not; at MENALCAS' hall
 There are bays enough for all.
 He, when young as we, did graze,
 But when old he planted bays.

Tomalin Here she comes; but with a look
 Far more catching than my hook;
 'Twas those eyes, I now dare swear,
 Led our lambs we know not where.

Hobbinol Not our lambs' own fleeces are
 Curled so lovely as her hair,
 Nor our sheep new-washed can be
 Half so white or sweet as she.

Phillis He so looks as fit to keep
 Somewhat else than silly sheep.

Hobbinol Come, let's in some carol new
 Pay to love and them their due.

All Joy to that happy pair
 Whose hopes united banish our despair.
  What shepherd could for love pretend,

Whilst all the nymphs on DAMON'S choice attend?
   What shepherdess could hope to wed
   Before MARINA'S turn were sped?
   Now lesser beauties may take place,
And meaner virtues come in play;
            While they,
            Looking from high,
            Shall grace
Our flocks and us with a propitious eye.
   But what is most, the gentle swain
   No more shall need of love complain;
   But virtue shall be beauty's hire,
And those be equal, that have equal fire.
   MARINA yields. Who dares be coy?
Or who despair, now DAMON does enjoy?
      Joy to that happy pair,
Whose hopes united banish our despair!

On the Victory Obtained by Blake

OVER THE SPANIARDS IN THE BAY OF SANTA CRUZ, IN THE ISLAND OF TENERIFFE, 1657

Now does Spain's fleet her spacious wings unfold,
Leaves the new world, and hastens for the old;
But though the wind was fair, they slowly swum,
Freighted with acted guilt, and guilt to come;
For this rich load, of which so proud they are,
Was raised by tyranny, and raised for war.
Every capacious galleon's womb was filled
With what the womb of wealthy kingdoms yield;
The new world's wounded entrails they had tore,
For wealth wherewith to wound the old once more;
Wealth which all others' avarice might cloy,
But yet in them caused as much fear as joy.
For now upon the main themselves they saw

That boundless empire, where you give the law;
Of wind's and water's rage they fearful be,
But much more fearful are your flags to see.
Day, that to those who sail upon the deep
More wished for and more welcome is than sleep,
They dreaded to behold, lest the sun's light
With English streamers should salute their sight;
In thickest darkness they would choose to steer,
So that such darkness might suppress their fear:
At length it vanishes, and fortune smiles,
For they behold the sweet Canary isles,
One of which doubtless is by Nature blessed
Above both worlds, since 'tis above the rest.
For lest some gloominess might stain her sky,
Trees there the duty of the clouds supply:
O noble trust which Heaven on this isle pours,
Fertile to be, yet never need her showers!
A happy people, which at once do gain
The benefits, without the ills, of rain!
Both health and profit Fate cannot deny,
Where still the earth is moist, the air still dry;
The jarring elements no discord know,
Fuel and rain together kindly grow;
And coolness there with heat does never fight,
This only rules by day, and that by night.
Your worth to all these isles a just right brings,
The best of lands should have the best of kings.
And these want nothing Heaven can afford,
Unless it be, the having you their lord;
But this great want will not a long one prove;
Your conquering sword will soon that want remove;
For Spain had better, she'll ere long confess,
Have broken all her swords, than this one peace;
Casting that league off, which she held so long,
She cast off that which only made her strong.
Forces and art, she soon will feel, are vain;
Peace, against you, was the sole strength of Spain;
By that alone those islands she secures,
Peace made them hers, but war will make them yours.
There the indulgent soil that rich grape breeds,

Which of the gods the fancied drink exceeds.
They still do yield, such is their precious mould,
All that is good, and are not cursed with gold;
With fatal gold, for still where that does grow
Neither the soil, nor people, quiet know;
Which troubles men to raise it when 'tis ore,
And when 'tis raised does trouble them much more.
Ah, why was thither brought that cause of war
Kind Nature had from thence removed so far!
In vain doth she those islands free from ill,
If Fortune can make guilty what she will.
But whilst I draw that scene, where you, ere long,
Shall conquests act, you present are unsung.

    For Santa Cruz the glad fleet takes her way;
And safely there casts anchor in the bay.
Never so many, with one joyful cry,
That place saluted, where they all must die.
Deluded men! Fate with you did but sport,
You 'scaped the sea, to perish in your port.
'Twas more for England's fame you should die there,
Where you had most of strength and least of fear.
The Peak's proud height the Spaniards all admire,
Yet in their breasts carry a pride much higher.
Only to this vast hill a power is given,
At once both to inhabit earth and heaven.
But this stupendous prospect did not near
Make them admire, so much as they did fear.

    For here they met with news, which did produce
A grief, above the cure of grape's best juice.
They learned with terror, that nor summer's heat,
Nor winter's storms, had made your fleet retreat.
To fight against such foes was vain, they knew,
Which did the rage of elements subdue,
Who on the ocean, that does horror give
To all beside, triumphantly do live.

    With haste they therefore all their galleons moor,
And flank with cannon from the neighbouring shore;
Forts, lines, and sconces, all the bay along,
They build, and act all that can make them strong.

    Fond men! who know not whilst such works they raise,

They only labour to exalt your praise.
Yet they by restless toil became at length
So proud and confident of their made strength,
That they with joy their boasting general heard
Wish then for that assault he lately feared.
His wish he has, for now undaunted Blake,
With wingèd speed, for Santa Cruz does make.
For your renown, the conquering fleet does ride
O'er seas as vast as is the Spaniard's pride.
Whose fleet and trenches viewed, he soon did say,
We to their strength are more obliged than they;
Wer't not for that, they from their fate would run,
And a third world seek out, our arms to shun.
Those forts, which there so high and strong appear,
Do not so much suppress, as show their fear.
Of speedy victory let no man doubt,
Our worst work's past, now we have found them out.
Behold their navy does at anchor lie,
And they are ours, for now they cannot fly.

    This said, the whole fleet gave it their applause,
And all assumes your courage, in your cause.
That bay they enter, which unto them owes
The noblest wreaths that victory bestows;
Bold Stayner leads; this fleet's designed by fate
To give him laurel, as the last did plate.

    The thundering cannon now begins the fight,
And, though it be at noon, creates a night;
The air was soon, after the fight begun,
Far more enflamed by it than by the sun.
Never so burning was that climate known;
War turned the temperate to the torrid zone.

    Fate these two fleets, between both worlds, had
        brought,
Who fight as if for both those worlds they fought.
Thousands of ways, thousands of men there die,
Some ships are sunk, some blown up in the sky.
Nature ne'er made cedars so high aspire
As oaks did then, urged by the active fire
Which, by quick powder's force, so high was sent
That it returned to its own element.

Torn limbs some leagues into the island fly,
Whilst others lower, in the sea, do lie;
Scarce souls from bodies severed are so far
By death, as bodies there were by the war.
The all-seeing sun ne'er gazed on such a sight;
Two dreadful navies there at anchor fight,
And neither have or power, or will, to fly;
There one must conquer, or there both must die.
Far different motives yet engaged them thus,
Necessity did them, but choice did us,
A choice which did the highest worth express,
And was attended by as high success;
For your resistless genius there did reign,
By which we laurels reaped e'en on the main.
So prosperous stars, though absent to the sense,
Bless those they shine for by their influence.

   Our cannon now tears every ship and sconce,
And o'er two elements triumphs at once.
Their galleons sunk, their wealth the sea does fill,
The only place where it can cause no ill.

   Ah! would those treasures which both Indias have
Were buried in as large and deep a grave!
War's chief support with them would buried be,
And the land owe her peace unto the sea.
Ages to come your conquering arms will bless,
There they destroy what had destroyed their peace;
And in one war the present age may boast
The certain seeds of many wars are lost.

   All the foe's ships destroyed by sea or fire,
Victorious Blake does from the bay retire.
His siege of Spain he then again pursues,
And there first brings of his success the news:
The saddest news that e'er to Spain was brought,
Their rich fleet sunk, and ours with laurel fraught;
Whilst Fame in every place her trumpet blows,
And tells the world how much to you it owes.

The Loyal Scot

UPON THE DEATH OF CAPTAIN DOUGLAS, BURNED ON HIS SHIP AT CHATHAM

Of the old heroes when the warlike shades
Saw Douglas marching on the Elysian glades,
They all, consulting, gathered in a ring,
Which of their poets should his welcome sing;
And, as a favourable penance, chose
Cleveland, on whom they would that task impose.
He understood, but willingly addressed
His ready muse, to court that noble guest.
Much had he cured the tumour of his vein,
He judged more clearly now and saw more plain;
For those soft airs had tempered every thought,
Since of wise Lethe he had drunk a draught.
Abruptly he begun, disguising art,
As of his satire this had been a part.

As so, brave Douglas, on whose lovely chin
The early down but newly did begin,
And modest beauty yet his sex did veil,
While envious virgins hope he is a male.
His yellow locks curl back themselves to seek,
Nor other courtship knew but to his cheek.
Oft as he in chill Esk or Tyne, by night,
Hardened and cooled his limbs, so soft, so white,
Among the reeds, to be espied by him,
The nymphs would rustle, he would forward swim.
They sighed, and said, Fond boy, why so untame,
That fly'st love's fires, reserved for other flame?

First on his ship he faced that horrid day,
And wondered much at those that ran away.
No other fear himself could comprehend,
Than lest Heaven fall ere thither he ascend:
But entertains the while his time, too short,
With birding at the Dutch, as if in sport;

Or waves his sword, and, could he them conjure
Within his circle, knows himself secure.
The fatal bark him boards with grappling fire,
And safely through its port the Dutch retire.
That precious life he yet disdains to save,
Or with known art to try the gentle wave.
Much him the honour of his ancient race
Inspired, nor would he his own deeds deface;
And secret joy in his calm soul does rise,
That Monck looks on to see how Douglas dies.
Like a glad lover the fierce flames he meets,
And tries his first embraces in their sheets;
His shape exact, which the bright flames enfold,
Like the sun's statue stands of burnished gold;
Round the transparent fire about him glows,
As the clear amber on the bee does close;
And, as on angels' heads their glories shine,
His burning locks adorn his face divine.
But when in his immortal mind he felt
His altering form and soldered limbs to melt,
Down on the deck he laid himself, and died,
With his dear sword reposing by his side,
And on the flaming plank so rests his head,
As one that warmed himself, and went to bed.
His ship burns down, and with his relics sinks,
And the sad stream beneath his ashes drinks.
Fortunate boy! if either pencil's fame,
Or if my verse can propagate thy name,
When Œta and Alcides are forgot,
Our English youth shall sing the valiant Scot.
  Skip saddles, Pegasus, thou needst not brag,
Sometimes the Galloway proves the better nag.
Shall not a death so generous, when told,
Unite our distance, fill our breaches old?
So in the Roman forum, Curtius brave,
Galloping down, closed up the gaping cave.
No more discourse of Scotch and English race,
Nor chant the fabulous hunt of Chevy-Chase;
Mixed in Corinthian metal at thy flame,
Our nations melting, thy Colossus frame.

Prick down the point, whoever has the art,
Where nature Scotland does from England part;
Anatomists may sooner fix the cells
Where life resides and understanding dwells.
But this we know, though that exceeds our skill,
That whosoever separates them does ill.
Will you the Tweed that sullen bounder call,
Of soil, of wit, of manners, and of all?
Why draw you not, as well, the thrifty line
From Thames, Trent, Humber, or at least the Tyne?
So may we the state-corpulence redress,
And little England, when we please, make less.
What ethic river is this wondrous Tweed,
Whose one bank virtue, t'other vice, does breed?
Or what new perpendicular does rise
Up from her streams, continued to the skies,
That between us the common air should bar,
And split the influence of every star?
But who considers right, will find indeed,
'Tis Holy Island parts us, not the Tweed.
Nothing but clergy could us two seclude,
No Scotch was ever like a bishop's feud.
All Litanies in this have wanted faith,
There's no *deliver us from a bishop's wrath*.
Never shall Calvin pardoned be for sales,
Never, for Burnet's sake, the Lauderdales;
For Becket's sake, Kent always shall have tails.
Who sermons e're can pacify and prayers?
Or to the joint stools reconcile the chairs?
Though kingdoms join, yet church will kick oppose;
The mitre still divides, the crown does close;
As in Rogation week they whip us round,
To keep in mind the Scotch and English bound.
What the ocean binds is by the bishops rent,
Then seas make islands in our continent.
Nature in vain us in one land compiles,
If the cathedral still shall have its isles.
Nothing, not bogs nor sands nor seas nor Alps,
Separates the world so as the bishops' scalps;
Stretch for the line their surcingle alone,

'Twill make a more unhabitable zone.
The friendly loadstone has not more combined,
Than bishops cramped the commerce of mankind.
Had it not been for such a bias strong,
Two nations ne'er had missed the mark so long.
The world in all doth but two nations bear,
The good, the bad, and these mixed everywhere;
Under each pole place either of these two,
The bad will basely, good will bravely, do;
And few, indeed, can parallel our climes,
For worth heroic, or heroic crimes.
The trial would, however, be too nice,
Which stronger were, a Scotch or English vice;
Or whether the same virtue would reflect,
From Scotch or English heart, the same effect.
Nation is all, but name, a Shibboleth,
Where a mistaken accent causes death.
In Paradise names only nature showed,
At Babel names from pride and discord flowed;
And ever since men, with a female spite,
First call each other names, and then they fight.
Scotland and England cause of just uproar;
Do man and wife signify rogue and whore?
Say but a Scot and straight we fall to sides;
That syllable like a Picts' wall divides.
Rational men's words pledges are of peace;
Perverted, serve dissension to increase.
For shame! extirpate from each loyal breast
That senseless rancour, against interest.
One king, one faith, one language, and one isle,
English and Scotch, 'tis all but cross and pile.
Charles, our great soul, this only understands;
He our affections both, and wills, commands;
And where twin-sympathies cannot atone,
Knows the last secret, how to make us one.

 Just so the prudent husbandman, that sees
The idle tumult of his factious bees,
The morning dews, and flowers, neglected grown,
The hive a comb-case, every bee a drone,

Powders them o'er, till none discerns his foes,
And all themselves in meal and friendship lose;
The insect kingdom straight begins to thrive,
And all work honey for the common hive
   Pardon, young hero, this so long transport,
Thy death more noble did the same extort.
My former satire for this verse forget,
My fault against my recantation set.
I single did against a nation write,
Against a nation thou didst singly fight.
My differing crimes do more thy virtue raise,
And, such my rashness, best thy valour praise.
   Here Douglas smiling said, he did intend,
After such frankness shown, to be his friend;
Forewarned him therefore, lest in time he were
Metempsychosed to some Scotch Presbyter.

An Horatian Ode

UPON CROMWELL'S RETURN FROM IRELAND

The forward youth that would appear,
Must now forsake his Muses dear,
       Nor in the shadows sing
       His numbers languishing:

'Tis time to leave the books in dust,
And oil the unusèd armour's rust;
       Removing from the wall
       The corselet of the hall.

So restless Cromwell could not cease
In the inglorious arts of peace,
       But through adventurous war
       Urgèd his active star;

And, like the three-forked lightning, first
Breaking the clouds where it was nursed,
       Did thorough his own side
       His fiery way divide:

(For 'tis all one to courage high,
The emulous, or enemy;
       And with such, to enclose,
       Is more than to oppose;)

Then burning through the air he went,
And palaces and temples rent;
       And Cæsar's head at last
       Did through his laurels blast.

'Tis madness to resist or blame
The face of angry Heaven's flame;
       And if we would speak true,
       Much to the man is due,

Who from his private gardens, where
He lived reservèd and austere,
      (As if his highest plot
      To plant the bergamot;)

Could by industrious valour climb
To ruin the great work of Time,
      And cast the kingdoms old,
      Into another mould;

Though Justice against Fate complain,
And plead the ancient rights in vain;
      (But those do hold or break,
      As men are strong or weak.)

Nature that hateth emptiness,
Allows of penetration less,
      And therefore must make room
      Where greater spirits come.

What field of all the civil war,
Where his were not the deepest scar?
      And Hampton shows what part
      He had of wiser art;

Where, twining subtle fears with hope,
He wove a net of such a scope
      That Charles himself might chase
      To Caresbrooke's narrow case,

That thence the royal actor borne,
The tragic scaffold might adorn;
      While round the armèd bands
      Did clap their bloody hands.

He nothing common did, or mean,
Upon that memorable scene,
      But with his keener eye
      The axe's edge did try;

Nor called the gods with vulgar spite
To vindicate his helpless right;
        But bowed his comely head
        Down, as upon a bed.

This was that memorable hour,
Which first assured the forcèd power;
        So, when they did design
        The capitol's first line,

A bleeding head, where they begun,
Did fright the architects to run;
        And yet in that the state
        Foresaw its happy fate.

And now the Irish are ashamed
To see themselves in one year tamed;
        So much one man can do,
        That does both act and know.

They can affirm his praises best,
And have, though overcome, confessed
        How good he is, how just,
        And fit for highest trust.

Nor yet grown stiffer with command,
But still in the republic's hand –
        How fit he is to sway,
        That can so well obey!

He to the Commons' feet presents
A kingdom for his first year's rents;
        And, what he may, forbears
        His fame, to make it theirs;

And has his sword and spoils ungirt,
To lay them at the public's skirt:
        So, when the falcon high
        Falls heavy from the sky,

She, having killed, no more doth search,
But on the next green bough to perch;
    Where, when he first does lure,
    The falconer has her sure.

What may not then our isle presume,
While victory his crest does plume?
    What may not others fear,
    If thus he crowns each year?

As Cæsar, he, ere long, to Gaul,
To Italy an Hannibal,
    And to all states not free,
    Shall climactèric be.

The Pict no shelter now shall find
Within his parti-coloured mind,
    But, from this valour sad,
    Shrink underneath the plaid;

Happy, if in the tufted brake,
The English hunter him mistake,
    Nor lay his hounds in near
    The Caledonian deer.

But thou, the war's and fortune's son,
March indefatigably on;
    And for the last effect,
    Still keep the sword erect;

Besides the force it has to fright
The spirits of the shady night,
    The same arts that did gain
    A power, must it maintain.

The First Anniversary

OF THE GOVERNMENT UNDER
HIS HIGHNESS THE LORD PROTECTOR

Like the vain curlings of the watery maze,
Which in smooth streams a sinking weight does raise,
So man, declining always, disappears
In the weak circles of increasing years;
And his short tumults of themselves compose,
While flowing time above his head does close.
    Cromwell alone, with greater vigour runs
(Sun-like) the stages of succeeding suns,
And still the day which he does next restore,
Is the just wonder of the day before;
Cromwell alone doth with new lustre spring,
And shines the jewel of the yearly ring.
'Tis he the force of scattered time contracts,
And in one year the work of ages acts;
While heavy monarchs made a wide return,
Longer and more malignant than Saturn;
And though they all Platonic years should reign,
In the same posture would be found again.
Their earthly projects under ground they lay,
More slow and brittle than the China clay;
Well may they strive to leave them to their son,
For one thing never was by one king done.
Yet some more active, for a frontier town
Took in by proxy, begs a false renown;
Another triumphs at the public cost,
And will have won, if he no more have lost;
They fight by others, but in person wrong,
And only are against their subjects strong;
Their other wars are but a feigned contest,
This common enemy is still opprest;
If conquerors, on them they turn their might,
If conquerèd, on them they wreak their spite;
They neither build the temple in their days,
Nor matter for succeeding founders raise;

Nor sacred prophecies consult within,
Much less themselves to perfect them begin;
No other care they bear of things above,
But with astrologers divine of Jove,
To know how long their planet yet reprieves
From their deservèd fate their guilty lives.
Thus (image-like) an useless time they tell,
And with vain sceptre strike the hourly bell;
Nor more contribute to the state of things,
Than wooden heads unto the viol's strings;
While indefatigable Cromwell hies,
And cuts his way still nearer to the skies,
Learning a music in the region clear,
To tune this lower to that higher sphere.

   So when Amphion did the lute command,
Which the god gave him, with his gentle hand,
The rougher stones, unto his measures hewed,
Danced up in order from the quarries rude;
This took a lower, that a higher place,
As he the treble altered, or the bass;
No note he struck, but a new story laid,
And the great work ascended while he played.

   The listening structures he with wonder eyed,
And still new stops to various time applied;
Now through the strings a martial rage he throws,
And joining straight the Theban tower arose;
Then as he strokes them with a touch more sweet,
The flocking marbles in a palace meet;
But for the most he graver notes did try,
Therefore the temples reared their columns high:
Thus, ere he ceased, his sacred lute creates
The harmonious city of the seven gates.

   Such was that wondrous order and consent,
When Cromwell tuned the ruling instrument;
While tedious statesmen many years did hack,
Framing a liberty that still went back;
Whose numerous gorge could swallow in an hour,
That island which the sea cannot devour:
Then our Amphion issues out and sings,
And once he struck and twice the powerful strings.

The Commonwealth then first together came,
And each one entered in the willing frame.
    All other matter yields, and may be ruled,
But who the minds of stubborn men can build?
No quarry bears a stone so hardly wrought,
Nor with such labour from its centre brought:
None to be sunk in the foundation bends,
Each in the house the highest place contends;
And each the hand that lays him will direct,
And some fall back upon the architect;
Yet all, composed by his attractive song,
Into the animated city throng.
    The Commonwealth does through their centres all
Draw the circumference of the public wall;
The crossest spirits here do take their part,
Fastening the contignation which they thwart:
And they whose nature leads them to divide,
Uphold, this one, and that the other side;
But the most equal still sustain the height,
And they, as pillars, keep the work upright,
While the resistance of opposèd minds
The fabric, as with arches, stronger binds;
Which, on the basis of a senate free,
Knit by the roof's protecting weight, agree.
    When for his foot he thus a place had found,
He hurls e'er since the world about him round;
And in his several aspects, like a star,
Here shines in peace, and thither shoots a war;
While by his beams observing princes steer,
And wisely court the influence they fear.
O, would they rather, by his pattern won,
Kiss the approaching, nor yet angry son,
And in their numbered footsteps humbly tread
The path where holy oracles do lead!
How might they under such a captain raise
The great designs kept for the latter days!
But mad with reason (so miscalled) of state,
They know them not, and what they know not, hate.
Hence still they sing Hosanna to the Whore,
And her, whom they should massacre, adore;

But Indians, whom they should convert, subdue,
Nor teach, but traffic with, or burn the Jew.
Unhappy princes, ignorantly bred,
By malice some, by error more misled,
If gracious Heaven to my life give length,
Leisure to time, and to my weakness strength,
Then shall I once with graver accents shake
Your regal sloth and your long slumbers wake;
Like the shrill huntsman that prevents the east,
Winding his horn to kings that chase the beast!

Till then my Muse shall halloo far behind
Angelic Cromwell, who outwings the wind,
And in dark nights, and in cold days, alone
Pursues the monster thorough every throne,
Which sinking to her Roman den impure,
Gnashes her gory teeth; nor there secure.

Hence oft I think, if in some happy hour
High grace should meet in one with highest power
And then a seasonable people still
Should bend to his, as he to Heaven's will,
What we might hope, what wonderful effect
From such a wished conjuncture might reflect!
Sure, the mysterious work, where none withstand,
Would forthwith finish under such a hand;
Foreshortened time its useless course would stay,
And soon precipitate the latest day:
But a thick cloud about that morning lies,
And intercepts the beams to mortal eyes;
That 'tis the most which we determine can,
If these the times, then this must be the man;
And well he therefore does, and well has guessed,
Who in his age has always forward pressed,
And knowing not where Heaven's choice may light,
Girds yet his sword, and ready stands to fight.
But men, alas! as if they nothing cared,
Look on, all unconcerned, or unprepared;
And stars still fall, and still the dragon's tail
Swinges the volumes of its horrid flail;
For the great justice that did first suspend
The world by sin, does by the same extend.

Hence that blest day still counterpoisèd wastes,
The ill delaying, what the elected hastes;
Hence, landing, Nature to new seas is tossed,
And good designs still with their authors lost.
  And thou, great Cromwell, for whose happy birth
A mould was chosen out of better earth, –
Whose saint-like mother we did lately see
Live out an age, long as a pedigree,
That she might seem, could we the fall dispute,
To have smelt the blossom, and not ate the fruit, –
Though none does of more lasting parents grow,
Yet never any did them honour so.
Though thou thine heart from evil still unstained,
And always hast thy tongue from fraud refrained;
Thou, who so oft through storms of thundering lead
Hast borne securely thine undaunted head;
Thy breast through poniarding conspiracies,
Drawn from the sheath of lying prophecies;
The proof beyond all other force or skill,
Our sins endanger, and shall one day kill.
How near they failed, and in thy sudden fall,
At once assayed to overturn us all!
Our brutish fury, struggling to be free,
Hurried thy horses, while they hurried thee;
When thou hadst almost quit thy mortal cares,
And soiled in dust thy crown of silver hairs.
  Let this one sorrow interweave among
The other glories of our yearly song;
Like skilful looms, which through the costly thread
Of purling ore, a shining wave do shed,
So shall the tears we on past grief employ,
Still as they trickle, glitter in our joy;
So with more modesty we may be true,
And speak, as of the dead, the praises due;
While impious men, deceived with pleasure short,
On their own hopes shall find the fall retort.
  But the poor beasts, wanting their noble guide,
(What could they more?) shrunk guiltily aside:
First wingèd fear transports them far away,
And leaden sorrow then their flight did stay.

See how they each their towering crests abate,
And the green grass and their known mangers hate,
Nor through wide nostrils snuff the wanton air,
Nor their round hoofs or curlèd manes compare;
With wandering eyes and restless ears they stood,
And with shrill neighings asked him of the wood.
    Thou, Cromwell, falling, not a stupid tree,
Or rock so savage, but it mourned for thee;
And all about was heard a panic groan,
As if that Nature's self were overthrown.
It seemed the earth did from the centre tear,
It seemed the sun was fallen out of the sphere:
Justice obstructed lay, and reason fooled,
Courage disheartened, and religion cooled;
A dismal silence through the palace went,
And then loud shrieks the vaulted marbles rent:
Such as the dying chorus sings by turns,
And to deaf seas and ruthless tempests mourns;
When now they sink, and now the plundering streams
Break up each deck and rip the oaken seams.
    But thee triumphant, hence, the fiery car
And fiery steeds had borne out of the war,
From the low world and thankless men, above
Unto the kingdom blest of peace and love:
We only mourned ourselves in thine ascent,
Whom thou hadst left beneath with mantle rent;
For all delight of life thou then didst lose,
When to command thou didst thyself depose,
Resigning up thy privacy so dear,
To turn the headstrong people's charioteer;
For to be Cromwell was a greater thing
Than aught below, or yet above, a king:
Therefore thou rather didst thyself depress,
Yielding to rule, because it made thee less.
    For neither didst thou from the first apply
Thy sober spirit unto things too high;
But in thine own fields exercisedst long
A healthful mind within a body strong;
Till at the seventh time, thou in the skies,
As a small cloud, like a man's hand didst rise;

Then did thick mists and winds the air deform,
And down at last thou pour'dst the fertile storm;
Which to the thirsty land did plenty bring,
But, though forewarned, o'ertook and wet the king.
   What since he did, an higher force him pushed
Still from behind, and it before him rushed.
Though undiscerned among the tumult blind,
Who think those high decrees by man designed,
'Twas Heaven would not that his power should cease,
But walk still middle betwixt war and peace;
Choosing each stone, and poising every weight,
Trying the measures of the breadth and height,
Here pulling down, and there erecting new,
Founding a firm state by proportions true.
   When Gideon so did from the war retreat,
Yet by the conquest of two kings grown great,
He on the peace extends a warlike power,
And Israel, silent, saw him rase the tower,
And how he Succoth's elders durst suppress
With thorns and briars of the wilderness;
No king might ever such a force have done,
Yet would not he be lord, nor yet his son.
   Thou with the same strength, and a heart so plain,
Didst, like thine olive, still refuse to reign;
Though why should others all thy labour spoil,
And brambles be anointed with thine oil?
Whose climbing flame, without a timely stop,
Had quickly levelled every cedar's top;
Therefore, first growing to thyself a law,
The ambitious shrubs thou in just time didst awe.
   So have I seen at sea, when whirling winds
Hurry the bark, but more the seamen's minds,
Who with mistaken course salute the sand,
And threatening rocks misapprehend for land, –
While baleful tritons to the shipwreck guide,
And corposants along the tacklings slide;
The passengers all wearied out before,
Giddy, and wishing for the fatal shore, –
Some lusty mate, who with more careful eye
Counted the hours, and every star did spy,

The helm does from the artless steersman strain,
And doubles back unto the safer main:
What though awhile they grumble, discontent?
Saving himself, he does their loss prevent.
    'Tis not a freedom that, where all command,
Nor tyranny, where one does them withstand;
But who of both the bounders knows to lay,
Him, as their father, must the State obey.
    Thou and thy house, like Noah's eight did rest,
Left by the war's flood, on the mountain's crest;
And the large vale lay subject to thy will,
Which thou but as an husbandman wouldst till;
And only didst for others plant the vine
Of liberty, not drunken with its wine.
    That sober liberty which men may have,
That they enjoy, but more they vainly crave;
And such as to their parent's tents do press,
May show their own, not see his nakedness.
    Yet such a Chammish issue still doth rage,
The shame and plague both of the land and age,
Who watched thy halting, and thy fall deride,
Rejoicing when thy foot had slipped aside,
That their new king might the fifth sceptre shake,
And make the world, by his example, quake;
Whose frantic army, should they want for men,
Might muster heresies, so one were ten.
What thy misfortune, they the Spirit call,
And their religion only is to fall.
O Mahomet! now couldst thou rise again,
Thy falling-sickness should have made thee reign;
While Feak and Simpson would in many a tome
Have writ the comments of thy sacred foam:
For soon thou mightst have passed among their rant,
Wer't but for thine unmovèd tulipant;
As thou must needs have owned them of thy band,
For prophecies fit to be alcoraned.
    Accursèd locusts, whom your king does spit
Out of the centre of the unbottomed pit;
Wanderers, adulterers, liars, Munzer's rest,
Sorcerers, atheists, Jesuits, possest;

You, who the Scriptures and the laws deface,
With the same liberty as points and lace;
O race, most hypocritically strict!
Bent to reduce us to the ancient Pict,
Well may you act the Adam and the Eve,
Ay, and the serpent too, that did deceive.
    But the great captain, now the danger's o'er,
Makes you, for his sake, tremble one fit more;
And, to your spite, returning yet alive,
Does with himself all that is good revive.
    So, when first man did through the morning new
See the bright sun his shining race pursue,
All day he followed, with unwearied sight,
Pleased with that other world of moving light;
But thought him, when he missed his sitting beams,
Sunk in the hills, or plunged below the streams,
While dismal blacks hung round the universe,
And stars, like tapers, burned upon his hearse;
And owls and ravens with their screeching noise
Did make the funerals sadder by their joys.
His weeping eyes the doleful vigils keep,
Not knowing yet the night was made for sleep.
Still to the west, where he him lost, he turned,
And with such accents, as despairing, mourned:
'Why did mine eyes once see so bright a ray?
Or why day last no longer than a day?'
When straight the sun behind him he descried,
Smiling serenely from the farther side.
    So while our star that gives us light and heat,
Seemed now a long and gloomy night to threat,
Up from the other world his flame doth dart,
And princes, shining through their windows, start;
Who their suspected counsellors refuse,
And credulous ambassadors accuse:
'Is this,' saith one, 'the nation that we read,
Spent with both wars, under a captain dead!
Yet rig a navy, while we dress us late,
And ere we dine, rase and rebuild a state?
What oaken forests, and what golden mines!
What mints of men, what union of designs!

Unless their ships do as their fowl proceed
Of shedding leaves, that with their ocean breed.
Theirs are not ships, but rather arks of war,
And beakèd promontories sailed from far;
Of floating islands a new hatchèd nest,
A fleet of worlds of other worlds in quest;
An hideous shoal of wood Leviathans,
Armed with three tire of brazen hurricanes,
That through the centre shoot their thundering side,
And sink the earth, that does at anchor ride.
What refuge to escape them can be found,
Whose watery leaguers all the world surround?
Needs must we all their tributaries be,
Whose navies hold the sluices of the sea!
The ocean is the fountain of command,
But that once took, we captives are on land;
And those that have the waters for their share,
Can quickly leave us neither earth nor air;
Yet if through these our fears could find a pass
Through double oak, and lined with treble brass;
That one man still, although but named, alarms
More than all men, all navies, and all arms;
Him all the day, him in late nights I dread,
And still his sword seems hanging o'er my head.
The nation had been ours, but his one soul
Moves the great bulk, and animates the whole.
He secrecy with number hath inchased,
Courage with age, maturity with haste;
The valiant's terror, riddle of the wise,
And still his falchion all our knots unties.
Where did he learn those arts that cost us dear?
Where below earth, or where above the sphere?
He seems a king by long succession born,
And yet the same to be a king does scorn.
Abroad a king he seems, and something more,
At home a subject on the equal floor.
O could I once him with our title see,
So should I hope yet he might die as we!
But let them write his praise that love him best,
It grieves me sore to have thus much confessed.'

Pardon, great Prince, if thus their fear or spite,
More than our love and duty do thee right;
I yield, nor further will the prize contend,
So that we both alike may miss our end;
While thou thy venerable head dost raise
As far above their malice as my praise;
And, as the angel of our commonweal,
Troubling the waters, yearly mak'st them heal.

A Poem

UPON THE DEATH OF HIS LATE HIGHNESS
THE LORD PROTECTOR

That Providence which had so long the care
Of Cromwell's head, and numbered every hair,
Now in itself (the glass where all appears)
Had seen the period of his golden years,
And henceforth only did attend to trace
What death might least so fair a life deface.
    The people, which, what most they fear, esteem,
Death when more horrid, so more noble deem,
And blame the last act, like spectators vain,
Unless the Prince, whom they applaud, be slain;
Nor fate indeed can well refuse the right
To those that lived in war, to die in fight.
    But long his valour none had left that could
Endanger him, or clemency that would;
And he (whom Nature all for peace had made,
But angry Heaven unto war had swayed,
And so less useful where he most desired,
For what he least affected was admired;)
Deservèd yet an end whose every part
Should speak the wondrous softness of his heart.
To Love and Grief the fatal writ was 'signed,
(Those nobler weaknesses of human kind,
From which those Powers that issued the decree,

Although immortal, found they were not free)
That they to whom his breast still open lies
In gentle passions, should his death disguise,
And leave succeeding ages cause to mourn,
As long as Grief shall weep, or Love shall burn.
    Straight does a slow and languishing disease,
Eliza, Nature's and his darling, seize;
Her, when an infant, taken with her charms,
He oft would flourish in his mighty arms,
And lest their force the tender burthen wrong,
Slacken the vigour of his muscles strong;
Then to the mother's breast her softly move,
Which, while she drained of milk, she filled with love.
But as with riper years her virtue grew,
And every minute adds a lustre new;
When with meridian height her beauty shined,
And thorough that sparkled her fairer mind;
When she with smiles serene, in words discreet,
His hidden soul at every turn could meet;
Then might you have daily his affection spied,
Doubling that knot which destiny had tied,
While they by sense, not knowing, comprehend
How on each other both their fates depend.
With her each day the pleasing hours he shares,
And at her aspect calms his growing cares;
Or with a grandsire's joy her children sees,
Hanging about her neck, or at his knees:
Hold fast, dear infants, hold them both, or none;
This will not stay, when once the other's gone.
A silent fire now wastes those limbs of wax,
And him within his tortured image racks.
So the flower withering, which the garden crowned,
The sad root pines in secret under ground.
Each groan he doubled, and each sigh she sighed,
Repeated over to the restless night;
No trembling string, composed to numbers new,
Answers the touch in notes more sad, more true.
She, lest he grieve, hides what she can, her pains;
And he, to lessen hers, his sorrow feigns;
Yet both perceived, yet both concealed their skills,

And so, diminishing, increased their ills,
That whether by each other's grief they fell,
Or on their own redoubled, none can tell.
    And now Eliza's purple locks were shorn,
Where she so long her father's fate had worn;
And frequent lightning, to her soul that flies,
Divides the air and opens all the skies.
And now his life, suspended by her breath,
Ran out impetuously to hastening Death.
Like polished mirrors, so his steely breast
Had every figure of her woes expressed,
And with the damp of her last gasps obscured,
Had drawn such stains as were not to be cured.
Fate could not either reach with single stroke,
But, the dear image fled, the mirror broke.
Who now shall tell us more of mournful swans,
Of halcyons kind, or bleeding pelicans?
No downy breast did e'er so gently beat,
Or fan with airy plumes so soft an heat;
For he no duty by his height excused,
Nor, though a prince, to be a man refused;
But rather than in his Eliza's pain
Not love, not grieve, would neither live nor reign;
And in himself so oft immortal tried,
Yet in compassion of another died.
    So have I seen a vine, whose lasting age,
Of many a winter hath survived the rage,
Under whose shady tent, men every year,
At its rich blood's expense, their sorrows cheer;
If some dear branch where it extends its life
Chance to be pruned by an untimely knife,
The parent tree unto the grief succeeds,
And through the wound its vital humour bleeds;
Trickling in watery drops, whose flowing shape
Weeps that it falls ere fixed into a grape;
So the dry stock, no more that spreading vine,
Frustrates the autumn, and the hopes of wine.
    A secret cause does sure those signs ordain,
Foreboding princes' falls, and seldom vain:
Whether some kinder powers, that wish us well,

What they above cannot prevent, foretell;
Or the great world do by consent presage,
As hollow seas with future tempests rage;
Or rather Heaven, which us so long foresees,
Their funerals celebrates, while it decrees.
But never yet was any human fate
By Nature solemnized with so much state:
He unconcerned the dreadful passage crossed,
But oh! what pangs that death did Nature cost!
   First the great thunder was shot off, and sent
The signal from the starry battlement:
The winds receive it, and its force outdo,
As practising how they could thunder too;
Out of the binder's hand the sheaves they tore,
And thrashed the harvest in the airy floor;
Or of huge trees, whose growth with his did rise,
The deep foundations opened to the skies;
Then heavy showers the wingèd tempests lead,
And pour the deluge o'er the chaos' head.
The race of warlike horses at his tomb
Offer themselves in many a hecatomb;
With pensive head towards the ground they fall,
And helpless languish at the tainted stall.
Numbers of men decrease with pains unknown,
And hasten (not to see his death) their own.
Such tortures all the elements unfixed,
Troubled to part where so exactly mixed;
And as through air his wasting spirits flowed,
The universe laboured beneath their load.
   Nature, it seemed, with him would nature vie,
He with Eliza, it with him would die.
   He without noise still travelled to his end,
As silent suns to meet the night descend;
The stars that for him fought, had only power
Left to determine now his fatal hour,
Which since they might not hinder, yet they cast
To choose it worthy of his glories past.
No part of time but bare his mark away
Of honour, – all the year was Cromwell's day;
But this, of all the most auspicious found,

Twice had in open field him victor crowned;
When up the armèd mountains of Dunbar
He marched, and through deep Severn, ending war:
What day should him eternize, but the same
That had before immortalized his name?
That so whoe'er would at his death have joyed,
In their own griefs might find themselves employed;
But those that sadly his departure grieved,
Yet joyed, remembering what he once achieved;
And the last minute his victorious ghost
Gave chase to Ligny on the Belgic coast:
Here ended all his mortal toils, he laid
And slept in peace under the laurel shade.

O Cromwell! Heaven's favourite, to none
Have such high honours from above been shown,
For whom the elements we mourners see,
And Heaven itself would the great herald be;
Which with more care set forth his obsequies
Than those of Moses, hid from human eyes;
As jealous only here, lest all be less
Than we could to his memory express.

Then let us too our course of mourning keep;
Where Heaven leads, 'tis piety to weep.
Stand back, ye seas, and shrunk beneath the veil
Of your abyss, with covered head bewail
Your monarch: we demand not your supplies
To compass-in our isle, – our tears suffice,
Since him away the dismal tempest rent,
Who once more joined us to the continent;
Who planted England on the Flanderic shore,
And stretched our frontier to the Indian ore;
Whose greater truths obscure the fables old,
Whether of British saints or worthies told,
And in a valour lessening Arthur's deeds,
For holiness the Confessor exceeds.

He first put arms into Religion's hand,
And timorous conscience unto courage manned;
The soldier taught that inward mail to wear,
And fearing God, how they should nothing fear;
Those strokes, he said, will pierce through all below,

Where those that strike from Heaven fetch their blow.
Astonished armies did their flight prepare,
And cities strong were stormèd by his prayer;
Of that for ever Preston's field shall tell
The story, and impregnable Clonmel,
And where the sandy mountain Fenwick scaled,
The sea between, yet hence his prayer prevailed.
What man was ever so in Heaven obeyed
Since the commanded sun o'er Gibeon stayed?
In all his wars needs must he triumph, when
He conquered God, still ere he fought with men:
Hence, though in battle none so brave or fierce,
Yet him the adverse steel could never pierce;
Pity it seemed to hurt him more, that felt
Each wound himself which he to others dealt,
Danger itself refusing to offend
So loose an enemy, so fast a friend.
Friendship, that sacred virtue, long does claim
The first foundation of his house and name:
But within one its narrow limits fall,
His tenderness extended unto all,
And that deep soul through every channel flows,
Where kindly Nature loves itself to lose.
More strong affections never reason served,
Yet still affected most what best deserved.
If he Eliza loved to that degree,
(Though who more worthy to be loved than she?)
If so indulgent to his own, how dear
To him the children of the Highest were!
For her he once did Nature's tribute pay;
For these his life adventured every day;
And 'twould be found, could we his thoughts have cast,
Their griefs struck deepest, if Eliza's last.
What prudence more than human did he need,
To keep so dear, so differing minds agreed?
The worser sort, so conscious of their ill,
Lie weak and easy to the ruler's will;
But to the good (too many or too few)
All law is useless, all reward is due.
Oh! ill-advised, if not for love, for shame,

Spare yet your own, if you neglect his fame;
Lest others dare to think your zeal a mask,
And you to govern only Heaven's task.
Valour, Religion, Friendship, Prudence died
At once with him, and all that's good beside;
And we, Death's refuge, Nature's dregs, confined
To loathsome life, alas! are left behind.
Where we (so once we used) shall now no more,
To fetch day, press about his chamber-door,
From which he issued with that awful state,
It seemed Mars broke through Janus' double gate;
Yet always tempered with an air so mild,
No April suns that e'er so gentle smiled;
No more shall hear that powerful language charm,
Whose force oft spared the labour of his arm;
No more shall follow where he spent the days
In war, in counsel, or in prayer and praise,
Whose meanest acts he would himself advance,
As ungirt David to the ark did dance.
All, all is gone of ours or his delight
In horses fierce, wild deer, or armour bright;
Francisca fair can nothing now but weep,
Nor with soft notes shall sing his cares asleep.
  I saw him dead: a leaden slumber lies,
And mortal sleep over those wakeful eyes;
Those gentle rays under the lids were fled,
Which through his looks that piercing sweetness shed;
That port, which so majestic was and strong,
Loose, and deprived of vigour, stretched along;
All withered, all discoloured, pale and wan,
How much another thing, no more that man!
O, human glory vain! O, Death! O, wings!
O, worthless world! O, transitory things!
Yet dwelt that greatness in his shape decayed,
That still though dead, greater than Death he laid,
And in his altered face you something feign
That threatens Death, he yet will live again.
Not much unlike the sacred oak, which shoots
To Heaven its branches, and through earth its roots;
Whose spacious boughs are hung with trophies round,

And honoured wreaths have oft the victor crowned;
When angry Jove darts lightning through the air
At mortal sins, nor his own plant will spare,
It groans and bruises all below, that stood
So many years the shelter of the wood;
The tree, erewhile foreshortened to our view,
When fallen shows taller yet than as it grew;
So shall his praise to after times increase,
When truth shall be allowed, and faction cease;
And his own shadows with him fall; the eye
Detracts from objects than itself more high;
But when Death takes them from that envied state,
Seeing how little, we confess how great.

    Thee, many ages hence, in martial verse
Shall the English soldier, ere he charge, rehearse;
Singing of thee, inflame himself to fight,
And, with the name of Cromwell, armies fright.
As long as rivers to the seas shall run,
As long as Cynthia shall relieve the sun,
While stags shall fly unto the forests thick,
While sheep delight the grassy downs to pick,
As long as future time succeeds the past,
Always thy honour, praise and name, shall last!

    Thou in a pitch how far beyond the sphere
Of human glory tower'st, and reigning there,
Despoiled of mortal robes, in seas of bliss
Plunging, dost bathe, and tread the bright abyss!
There thy great soul yet once a world doth see,
Spacious enough and pure enough for thee.
How soon thou Moses hast, and Joshua found,
And David, for the sword and harp renowned;
How straight canst to each happy mansion go,
(Far better known above than here below,)
And in those joys dost spend the endless day,
Which in expressing, we ourselves betray!

    For we, since thou art gone, with heavy doom,
Wander like ghosts about thy lovèd tomb,
And lost in tears, have neither sight nor mind
To guide us upward through this region blind;
Since thou art gone, who best that way couldst teach,

Only our sighs, perhaps, may thither reach.
   And Richard yet, where his great parent led,
Beats on the rugged track: he virtue dead
Revives, and by his milder beams assures;
And yet how much of them his grief obscures!
He, as his father, long was kept from sight
In private, to be viewed by better light;
But opened once, what splendour does he throw!
A Cromwell in an hour a prince will grow.
How he becomes that seat, how strongly strains,
How gently winds at once the ruling reins!
Heaven to this choice prepared a diadem,
Richer than any Eastern silk, or gem,
A pearly rainbow, where the sun inchased,
His brows, like an imperial jewel graced.
   We find already what those omens mean,
Earth ne'er more glad, nor Heaven more serene.
Cease now our griefs, calm peace succeeds a war,
Rainbows to storms, Richard to Oliver.
Tempt not his clemency to try his power,
He threats no deluge, yet foretells a shower.

SATIRES

Flecknoe, an English Priest at Rome

Obliged by frequent visits of this man,
Whom as priest, poet, and musician,
I for some branch of Melchisèdek took,
(Though he derives himself from my Lord Brooke),
I sought his lodging, which is at the sign
Of the sad Pelican, – subject divine
For poetry: there, three stair-cases high,
Which signifies his triple property,
I found at last a chamber, as 'twas said,
But seemed a coffin set on the stair's head;
Not higher than seven, nor larger than three feet;
Only there was nor ceiling, nor a sheet,
Save that the ingenious door did, as you come,
Turn in, and show to wainscot half the room:
Yet of his state no man could have complained,
There being no bed where he entertained;
And though within one cell so narrow pent,
He'd stanzas for a whole apartement.
    Straight without farther information,
In hideous verse, he, in a dismal tone,
Begins to exorcise, as if I were
Possessed, – and sure the devil brought me there.
But I, who now imagined myself brought
To my last trial, in a serious thought
Calmed the disorders of my youthful breast,
And to my martyrdom preparèd rest.
Only this frail ambition did remain,
The last distemper of the sober brain,
That there had been some present to assure
The future ages how I did endure;

And how I, silent, turned my burning ear
Towards the verse, and when that could not hear,
Held him the other, and unchangèd yet,
Asked still for more and prayed him to repeat;
Till the tyrant, weary to persecute,
Left off, and tried to allure me with his lute.

   Now as two instruments to the same key
Being tuned by art, if the one touchèd be,
The other opposite as soon replies,
Moved by the air and hidden sympathies;
So while he with his gouty fingers crawls
Over the lute, his murmuring belly calls,
Whose hungry guts, to the same straitness twined,
In echo to the trembling strings repined.

   I that perceived now what his music meant,
Asked civilly, if he had eat this Lent?
He answered, yes; with such, and such a one;
For he has this of generous, that alone
He never feeds, save only when he tries
With gristly tongue to dart the passing flies.
I asked if he eat flesh, and he, that was
So hungry, that though ready to say mass,
Would break his fast before, said he was sick,
And the ordinance was only politic.
Nor was I longer to invite him, scant
Happy at once to make him Protestant
And silent. Nothing now dinner stayed,
But till he had himself a body made,
I mean till he were dressed; for else so thin
He stands, as if he only fed had been
With consecrated wafers, and the Host
Hath sure more flesh and blood than he can boast;
This basso-relievo of a man –
Who, as a camel tall, yet easily can
The needle's eye thread without any stitch
(His only impossible is to be rich,) –
Lest his too subtle body, growing rare,
Should leave his soul to wander in the air,
He therefore circumscribes himself in rhymes,
And swaddled in's own papers seven times,

Wears a close jacket of poetic buff,
With which he doth his third dimension stuff.
Thus armèd underneath, he over all
Does make a primitive sottana fall,
And above that yet casts an antique cloak,
Worn at the first council of Antioch,
Which by the Jews long hid, and disesteemed,
He heard of by tradition, and redeemed.
But were he not in this black habit decked,
This half-transparent man would soon reflect
Each colour that he passed by, and be seen,
As the chameleon, yellow, blue, or green.

   He dressed, and ready to disfurnish now
His chamber, whose compactness did allow
No empty place for complimenting doubt,
But who came last is forced first to go out;
I met one on the stairs who made me stand,
Stopping the passage, and did him demand;
I answered, 'He is here, Sir, but you see
You cannot pass to him but thorough me.'
He thought himself affronted, and replied,
'I, whom the palace never has denied,
Will make the way here;' I said, 'Sir, you'll do
Me a great favour, for I seek to go.'
He, gathering fury, still made sign to draw,
But himself there closed in a scabbard saw
As narrow as his sword's; and I that was
Delighted, said, 'There can no body pass
Except by penetration hither, where
Two make a crowd, nor can three persons here
Consist but in one substance.' Then, to fit
Our peace, the priest said I too had some wit;
To prov't, I said, 'The place doth us invite,
By its own narrowness, Sir, to unite.'
He asked me pardon; and to make me way
Went down, as I him followed to obey.
But the propitiatory priest had straight
Obliged us, when below, to celebrate
Together our atonement; so increased
Betwixt us two, the dinner to a feast.

Let it suffice that we could eat in peace,
And that both poems did, and quarrels, cease
During the table, though my new-made friend
Did, as he threatened, ere 'twere long intend
To be both witty and valiant; I loath,
Said 'twas too late, he was already both.

But, now, alas! my first tormentor came,
Who, satisfied with eating, but not tame,
Turns to recite: though judges most severe,
After the assizes' dinner, mild appear,
And on full stomach do condemn but few,
Yet he more strict my sentence doth renew,
And draws out of the black box of his breast
Ten quire of paper, in which he was dressed.
Yet that which was a greater cruelty
Than Nero's poem, he calls charity:
And so the Pelican, at his door hung,
Picks out the tender bosom to its young.

Of all his poems there he stands ungirt,
Save only two foul copies for his shirt;
Yet these he promises as soon as clean:
But how I loathed to see my neighbour glean
Those papers, which he peeled from within
Like white flakes rising from a leper's skin!
More odious than those rags which the French youth
At ordinaries after dinner show'th,
When they compare their chancres and poulains!
Yet he first kissed them, and after takes pains
To read, and then, because he understood
Not one word, thought and swore that they were good.
But all his praises could not now appease
The provoked author, whom it did displease
To hear his verses, by so just a curse,
That were ill made, condemned to be read worse:
And how (impossible!) he made yet more
Absurdities in them than were before;
For he his untuned voice did fall or raise
As a deaf man upon a viol plays,
Making the half-points and the periods run
Confuseder than the atoms in the sun.

Thereat the poet swelled with anger full,
And roared out like Perillus in's own bull:
'Sir, you read false.' 'That, any one, but you,
Should know the contrary.' Whereat, I now
Made mediator in my room, said, 'Why?
To say that you read false, Sir, is no lie.'
Thereat the waxen youth relented straight,
But saw with sad despair that 'twas too late;
For the disdainful poet was retired
Home, his most furious satire to have fired
Against the rebel; who, at this struck dead,
Wept bitterly as disinherited.
Who should commend his mistress now? Or who
Praise him? Both difficult indeed to do
With truth. I counselled him to go in time,
Ere the fierce poet's anger turned to rhyme.
   He hasted; and I, finding myself free,
As one 'scaped strangely from captivity,
Have made the chance be painted; and go now
To hang it in Saint Peter's for a vow.

Tom May's Death

As one put drunk into the packet-boat,
TOM MAY was hurried thence, and did not know't;
But was amazed on the Elysian side,
And, with an eye uncertain gazing wide,
Could not determine in what place he was,
(For whence, in Steven's alley, trees or grass?)
Nor where the Pope's Head, nor the Mitre lay,
Signs by which still he found and lost his way.
At last, while doubtfully he all compares,
He saw near hand, as he imagined, ARES.
Such did he seem for corpulence and port,
But 'twas a man much of another sort;
'Twas BEN, that in the dusky laurel shade,
Amongst the chorus of old poets, laid,
Sounding of ancient heroes, such as were
The subject's safety, and the rebel's fear;
And how a double-headed vulture eats
BRUTUS and CASSIUS, the people's cheats;
But, seeing MAY, he varied straight his song,
Gently to signify that he was wrong.
Cups more than civil of Emathian wine,
I sing (said he) and the Pharsalian sign,
Where the historian of the Commonwealth
In his own bowels sheathed the conquering health.
By this MAY to himself and them was come;
He found he was translated, and by whom;
Yet then with foot as stumbling as his tongue,
Pressed for his place among the learnèd throng;
But BEN, who knew not neither foe nor friend,
Sworn enemy to all that do pretend,
Rose more than ever he was seen severe,
Shook his gray locks, and his own bays did tear
At this intrusion; then, with laurel wand,
The awful sign of his supreme command,
At whose dread whisk VIRGIL himself does quake,
And HORACE patiently its stroke doth take,
As he crowds in, he whipped him o'er the pate,

Like PEMBROKE at the masque, and then did rate:
  'Far from these blessed shades tread back again,
Most servile wit, and mercenary pen.
Polydore, Lucan, Alan, Vandal, Goth,
Malignant poet and historian both.
Go seek the novice statesmen and obtrude
On them some Roman cast similitude;
Tell them of liberty, the stories fine,
Until you all grow consuls in your wine,
Or thou, dictator of the glass, bestow
On him the CATO, this the CICERO,
Transferring old Rome hither in your talk,
As BETHLEM'S house did to LORETTO walk.
Foul architect! that hadst not eye to see
How ill the measures of these states agree,
And who by Rome's example England lay,
Those but to LUCAN do continue MAY;
But thee, nor ignorance, nor seeming good
Misled, but malice fixed and understood.
Because some one than thee more worthy wears
The sacred laurel, hence are all these tears.
Must therefore all the world be set on flame
Because a Gazette-writer missed his aim?
And for a tankard-bearing muse must we,
As for the basket, Guelphs and Ghibelines be?
When the sword glitters o'er the judge's head,
And fear has coward churchmen silencèd,
Then is the poet's time, 'tis then he draws,
And single fights forsaken virtue's cause.
He, when the wheel of empire whirleth back,
And though the world's disjointed axle crack,
Sings still of ancient rights and better times,
Seeks wretched good, arraigns successful crimes;
But thou, base man, first prostituted hast
Our spotless knowledge and the studies chaste,
Apostatizing from our arts and us,
To turn the chronicler to SPARTACUS;
Yet wast thou taken hence with equal fate,
Before thou couldst great CHARLES his death relate,
But what will deeper wound thy little mind,

Hast left surviving DAVENANT still behind,
Who laughs to see, in this thy death, renewed
Right Roman poverty and gratitude.
Poor poet thou, and grateful senate they,
Who thy last reckoning did so largely pay,
And with the public gravity would come,
When thou hadst drunk thy last, to lead thee home,
If that can be thy home where SPENSER lies,
And reverend CHAUCER; but their dust does rise
Against thee, and expels thee from their side,
As the eagle's plumes from other birds divide:
Nor here thy shade must dwell; return, return,
Where sulphury PHLEGETHON does ever burn!
There CERBERUS with all his jaws shall gnash,
MEGÆRA thee with all her serpents lash;
Thou, riveted unto IXION's wheel,
Shalt break, and the perpetual vulture feel!
'Tis just what torments poets e'er did feign,
Thou first historically shouldst sustain.'

Thus, by irrevocable sentence cast,
MAY only master of these revels passed;
And straight he vanished in a cloud of pitch,
Such as unto the Sabbath bears the witch.

The Character of Holland

Holland, that scarce deserves the name of land,
As but the off-scouring of the British sand,
And so much earth as was contributed
By English pilots when they heaved the lead,
Or what by the ocean's slow alluvion fell
Of shipwrecked cockle and the mussel-shell, –
This indigested vomit of the sea
Fell to the Dutch by just propriety.

　　Glad then, as miners that have found the ore,
They, with mad labour, fished the land to shore,
And dived as desperately for each piece
Of earth, as if't had been of ambergris,
Collecting anxiously small loads of clay,
Less than what building swallows bear away,
Or than those pills which sordid beetles roll,
Transfusing into them their dunghill soul.

　　　　How did they rivet with gigantic piles,
Thorough the centre their new-catchèd miles?
And to the stake a struggling country bound,
Where barking waves still bait the forcèd ground,
Building their watery Babel far more high
To reach the sea, than those to scale the sky!

　　Yet still his claim the injured ocean laid,
And oft at leap-frog o'er their steeples played,
As if on purpose it on land had come
To show them what's their *mare liberum*.
A daily deluge over them does boil;
The earth and water play at level coil.
The fish ofttimes the burgher dispossessed,
And sat, not as a meat, but as a guest,
And oft the Tritons and the sea-nymphs saw
Whole shoal of Dutch served up for cabillau;
Or, as they over the new level ranged
For pickled herring, pickled *heeren* changed.
Nature, it seemed, ashamed of her mistake,
Would throw their land away at duck and drake;
Therefore necessity, that first made kings,

Something like government among them brings;
For, as with pygmies, who best kills the crane,
Among the hungry he that treasures grain,
Among the blind the one-eyed blinkard reigns,
So rules among the drownèd he that drains:
Not who first sees the rising sun, commands,
But who could first discern the rising lands;
Who best could know to pump an earth so leak,
Him they their Lord, and Country's Father, speak;
To make a bank, was a great plot of state;
Invent a shovel, and be magistrate.
Hence some small dyke-grave, unperceived, invades
The power, and grows, as 'twere, a king of spades;
But, for less envy, some joint states endures,
Who look like a commission of the sewers:
For these Half-anders, half wet, and half dry,
Nor bear strict service, nor pure liberty.
  'Tis probable religion, after this,
Came next in order, which they could not miss;
How could the Dutch but be converted, when
The Apostles were so many fishermen?
Besides, the waters of themselves did rise,
And, as their land, so them did re-baptize.
Though Herring for their God few voices missed,
And Poor-John to have been the Evangelist.
Faith, that could never twins conceive before,
Never so fertile, spawned upon this shore,
More pregnant than their Margaret, that laid down
For Hans-in-Kelder of a whole Hans-Town.
  Sure when religion did itself embark,
And from the east would westward steer its ark,
It struck, and splitting on this unknown ground,
Each one thence pillaged the first piece he found;
Hence Amsterdam, Turk-Christian-Pagan-Jew;
Staple of sects, and mint of schism grew;
That bank of conscience, where not one so strange
Opinion but finds credit, and exchange.
In vain for Catholics ourselves we bear;
The universal church is only there.
Nor can civility there want for tillage,

Where wisely for their Court they chose a village;
How fit a title clothes their governors,
Themselves the Hogs, as all their subjects boors!
  Let it suffice to give their country fame,
That it had one Civilis called by name,
Some fifteen hundred and more years ago,
But surely never any that was so.
  See but their mermaids, with their tails of fish,
Reeking at church over the chafing-dish!
A vestal turf, enshrined in earthern ware,
Fumes through the loopholes of a wooden square;
Each to the temple with these altars tend,
(But still does place it at her western end;)
While the fat steam of female sacrifice
Fills the priest's nostrils, and puts out his eyes.
  Or what a spectacle the skipper gross,
A water Hercules, butter Coloss,
Tunned up with all their several towns of beer;
When, staggering upon some land, snick and sneer,
They try, like statuaries, if they can,
Cut out each other's Athos to a man,
And carve in their large bodies, where they please,
The arms of the United Provinces
  But when such amity at home is showed,
What then are their confederacies abroad?
Let this one courtesy witness all the rest,
When their whole navy they together pressed,
Not Christian captives to redeem from bands,
Or intercept the western golden sands,
No, but all ancient rights and leagues must vail,
Rather than to the English strike their sail;
To whom their weather-beaten province owes
Itself, when, as some greater vessel tows
A cock-boat, tossed with the same wind and fate,
We buoyed so often up their sinking state.
Was this *jus belli et pacis*? Could this be
Cause why their burgomaster of the sea,
Rammed with gunpowder, flaming with brand-wine,
Should raging hold his linstock to the mine?
While, with feigned treaties, they invade by stealth

Our sore new-circumcisèd commonwealth.
Yet of his vain attempt no more he sees,
Than of case-butter shot, and bullet cheese;
And the torn navy staggered with him home,
While the sea laughed itself into a foam.
'Tis true, since that, (as fortune kindly sports)
A wholesome danger drove us to our ports,
While half their banished keels the tempest tossed,
Half bound at home in prison to the frost;
That ours, meantime, at leisure might careen,
In a calm winter, under skies serene,
As the obsequious air and waters rest,
Till the dear Halcyon hatch out all its nest.
The commonwealth doth by its losses grow,
And, like its own seas, only ebbs to flow;
Besides, that very agitation laves,
And purges out the corruptible waves.
    And now again our armèd Bucentaur
Doth yearly their sea-nuptials restore;
And now the Hydra of seven provinces
Is strangled by our infant Hercules.
Their tortoise wants its vainly stretchèd neck,
Their navy, all our conquest, or our wreck;
Or, what is left, their Carthage overcome,
Would render fain unto our better Rome;
Unless our senate, lest their youth disuse
The war (but who would?), peace, if begged, refuse.
For now of nothing may our state despair,
Darling of Heaven, and of men the care,
Provided that they be, what they have been,
Watchful abroad, and honest still within.
For while our Neptune doth a trident shake,
Steeled with those piercing heads, Deane, Monck, and
        Blake,
And while Jove governs in the highest sphere,
Vainly in hell let Pluto domineer.

The Last Instructions to a Painter
about the Dutch Wars, 1667

After two sittings, now our Lady State,
To end her picture, does the third time wait;
But ere thou fall'st to work, first, Painter, see,
If't ben't too slight grown or too hard for thee.
Canst thou paint without colours? Then 'tis right:
For so we too without a fleet can fight.
Or canst thou daub a sign-post, and that ill?
'Twill suit our great debauch, and little skill.
Or hast thou marked how antique masters limn
The alley-roof with snuff of candle dim,
Sketching in shady smoke prodigious tools?
'Twill serve this race of drunkards, pimps, and fools.
But if to match our crimes thy skill presumes,
As the Indians draw our luxury in plumes,
Or if to score out our compendious fame,
With Hooke then through your microscope take aim,
Where, like the new Comptroller, all men laugh,
To see a tall louse brandish a white staff;
Else shalt thou oft thy guiltless pencil curse,
Stamp on thy pallet, not perhaps the worse.
The painter so long having vexed his cloth,
Of his hound's mouth to feign the raging froth,
His desperate pencil at the work did dart;
His anger reached that rage which passed his art;
Chance finished that, which art could but begin,
And he sat smiling how his dog did grin;
So may'st thou perfect by a lucky blow,
What all thy softest touches cannot do.
    Paint then St Albans full of soup and gold,
The new Court's pattern, stallion of the old;
Him neither wit nor courage did exalt,
But Fortune chose him for her pleasure's salt.
Paint him with drayman's shoulders, butcher's mien,
Membered like mule, with elephantine chin.
Well he the title of St Albans bore,

For never Bacon studied nature more;
But age, allaying now that youthful heat,
Fits him in France to play at cards, and treat.
  Draw no commission, lest the Court should lie,
And, disavowing treaty, ask supply.
He needs no seal but to St James's lease,
Whose breeches were the instruments of peace;
Who, if the French dispute his power, from thence
Can straight produce them a plenipotence.
Nor fears he the Most Christian should trepan
Two saints at once, St German and Alban;
But thought the golden age was now restored,
When men and women took each other's word.
  Paint then again her Highness to the life,
Philosopher beyond Newcastle's wife.
She naked can Archimedes' self put down,
For an experiment upon the crown.
She perfected that engine oft essayed,
How after child-birth to renew a maid;
And found how royal heirs might be matured
In fewer months than mothers once endured.
Hence Crowder made the rare inventress free
Of's Highness's Royal Society.
Happiest of women if she were but able
To make her glassen Duke once malleable.
Paint her with oyster-lip, and breath of fame,
Wide mouth, that sparagus may well proclaim;
With chancellor's belly, and so large a rump,
Where (not behind the coach) her pages jump.
Express her studying now, if China clay
Can, without breaking, venomed juice convey:
Or how a mortal poison she may draw
Out of the cordial meal of the cocoa.
Witness ye stars of night, and thou the pale
Moon, that o'ercome with the sick steam, didst fail:
Ye neighbouring elms, which your green leaves did shed,
And fawns which from the womb abortive fled.
Not unprovoked she tries forbidden arts,
But in her soft breast love's hid cancer smarts;
While she resolves at once Sidney's disgrace,

And herself scorned for emulous Denham's face;
And nightly hears the hated guard, away
Galloping with the Duke to other prey.

    Paint Castlemaine in colours which will hold
Her, not her picture, for she now grows old.
She through her lackey's drawers, as he ran,
Discerned love's cause, and a new flame began.
Her wonted joys thenceforth, and Court, she shuns,
And still within her mind the footman runs;
His brazen calves, his brawny thighs, (the face
She slights) his feet shaped for a smoother race!
Then, poring with her glass, she re-adjusts
Her locks, and oft-tired beauty now distrusts;
Fears lest he scorned a woman once assayed,
And now first wished she e'er had been a maid.
Great Love! how dost thou triumph, and how reign,
That to a groom couldst humble her disdain!
Stripped to her skin, see how she stooping stands,
Nor scorns to rub him down with those fair hands,
And washing (lest the scent her crime disclose)
His sweaty hoofs, tickles him 'twixt the toes.
But envious fame too soon began to note
More gold in's fob, more lace upon his coat;
And he unwary, and of tongue too fleet,
No longer could conceal his fortune sweet.
Justly the rogue was whipped in Porter's den,
And Jermyn straight has leave to come again.
Ah, Painter! now could Alexander live,
And this Campaspe the Apelles give!

    Draw next a pair of tables opening, then
The House of Commons clattering like the men.
Describe the Court and country both set right
On opposite points, the black against the white;
Those having lost the nation at trick-track,
These now adventuring how to win it back.
The dice betwixt them must the fate divide,
As chance does still in multitudes decide.
But here the Court doth its advantage know,
For the cheat, Turner, for them both must throw;
As some from boxes, he so from the chair

Can strike the die, and still with them go share.
  Here, Painter, rest a little and survey
With what small arts the public game they play;
For so too, Rubens, with affairs of state,
His labouring pencil oft would recreate.
  The close Cabal marked how the navy eats,
And thought all lost that goes not to the cheats:
So therefore secretly for peace decrees,
Yet for a war the Parliament would squeeze;
And fix to the revenue such a sum
Should Goodrick silence, and make Paston dumb,
Should pay land armies, should dissolve the vain
Commons, and ever such a Court maintain,
Hyde's avarice, Bennet's luxury, should suffice,
And what can these defray but the excise?
Excise, a monster worse than e'er before
Frighted the midwife, and the mother tore.
A thousand hands she has, a thousand eyes,
Breaks into shops, and into cellars pries;
With hundred rows of teeth the shark exceeds,
And on all trades, like casawar, she feeds;
Chops off the piece where'er she close the jaw,
Else swallows all down her indented maw.
She stalks all day in streets, concealed from sight,
And flies like bats with leathern wings by night;
She wastes the country, and on cities preys.
Her, of a female harpy in dog-days,
Black Birch, of all the earth-born race most hot,
And most rapacious, like himself begot;
And of his brat enamoured, as't increased,
Buggered in incest with the mongrel beast.
  Say, Muse, for nothing can escape thy sight,
(And Painter, wanting other, draw this fight,)
Who in an English senate fierce debate
Could raise so long, for this new whore of State.
  Of early wittols first the troop marched in,
For diligence renowned, and discipline;
In loyal haste they left young wives in bed,
And Denham these with one consent did head.
  Of the old courtiers next a squadron came,

Who sold their master, led by Ashburnham.
    To them succeeds a despicable rout,
But knew the word, and well could face about;
Expectants pale, with hopes of spoil allured,
Though yet but pioneers, and led by Steward.
    Then damning cowards ranged the vocal plain;
Wood these commands, knight of the horn and cane:
Still his hook-shoulder seems the blow to dread,
And under's arm-pit he defends his head.
The posture strange men laugh at, of his poll
Hid with his elbow like the spice he stole;
Headless St Dennis so his head does bear,
And both of them alike French martyrs were.
    Court officers, as used, the next place took,
And followed Fox, but with disdainful look;
His birth, his youth, his brokage, all dispraise
In vain, for always he commands that pays.
    Then the procurers under Prodgers filed,
Gentlest of men, and his lieutenant mild,
Bronkard, love's squire; through all the field arrayed,
No troop was better clad, nor so well paid.
    Then marched the troop of Clarendon, all full,
Haters of fowl, to teal preferring bull;
Gross bodies, grosser minds, and grosser cheats;
And bloated Wren conducts them to their seats.
    Charlton advances next (whose coife does awe
The mitred troop) and with his looks gives law.
He marched with beaver cocked of bishop's brim,
And hid much fraud under an aspect grim.
    Next do the lawyers, sordid band, appear,
Finch in the front, and Thurland in the rear.
    The troop of privilege, a rabble bare
Of debtors deep, fell to Trelawney's care;
Their fortune's error they supplied in rage,
Nor any farther would than these engage.
    Then marched the troop, whose valiant acts before
(Their public acts), obliged them to do more,
For chimney's sake they all Sir Pool obeyed,
Or, in his absence, him that first it laid.
    Then came the thrifty troop of privateers,

Whose horses each with other interferes:
Before them Higgins rides with brow compact,
Mourning his Countess, anxious for his Act.
    Sir Frederick and Sir Solomon draw lots,
For the command of politics or Scots;
Thence fell to words; but quarrels to adjourn,
Their friends agreed they should command by turn.
    Carteret the rich did the accountants guide,
And in ill English all the world defied.
    The Papists (but of those the house had none
Else) Talbot offered to have led them on.
    Bold Duncombe next, of the projectors chief,
And old Fitz Harding of the Eaters Beef.
    Late and disordered out the drunkards drew,
Scarce them their leaders, they their leaders knew.
    Before them entered, equal in command,
Apsley and Brotherick marching hand in hand.
    Last then but one, Powell, that could not ride,
Led the French standard weltering in his stride;
He, to excuse his slowness, truth confessed,
That 'twas so long before he could be dressed.
    The lord's sons last all these did reinforce,
Cornbury before them managed hobby-horse.
    Never before nor since an host so steeled
Trooped on to muster in the Tuttle-field.
    Not the first cock-horse that with cork was shod
To rescue Albemarle from the sea-cod:
Nor the late feather-men, whom Tomkins fierce
Shall with one breath like thistle-down disperse.
    All the two Coventrys their generals chose,
For one had much, the other nought to lose.
Not better choice all accidents could hit,
While hector Harry steers by Will the wit.
They both accept the charge with merry glee,
To fight a battle from all gunshot free.
Pleased with their numbers, yet in valour wise,
They feigned a parley, better to surprise;
They who ere long shall the rude Dutch upbraid,
Who in a time of treaty durst invade.
    Thick was the morning, and the House was thin,

The Speaker early, when they all fell in.
Propitious heavens! had not you them crossed,
Excise had got the day, and all been lost:
For t'other side all in loose quarters lay
Without intelligence, command or pay;
A scattered body, which the foe ne'er tried,
But often did among themselves divide.
And some run o'er each night, while others sleep,
And undescried returned 'fore morning peep.
But Strangways, who all night still walked the round,
For vigilance and courage both renowned,
First spied the enemy, and gave the alarm,
Fighting it single till the rest might arm;
Such Roman Cocles strid before the foe,
The failing bridge behind, the streams below.
Each ran as chance him guides to several post,
And all to pattern his example, boast;
Their former trophies they recall to mind,
And to new edge their angry courage, grind.
  First entered forward Temple, conqueror
Of Irish cattle, and solicitor.
Then daring Seymour, that with spear and shield
Had stretched the monster patent on the field.
Keen Whorwood next in aid of damsel frail,
That pierced the giant Mordaunt through his mail:
And surly Williams the accountant's bane,
And Lovelace young of chimney-men the cane.
Old Waller, trumpet-general, swore he'd write
This combat truer than the naval fight.
Of birth, state, wit, strength, courage, Howard presumes,
And in his breast wears many Montezumes.
These, with some more, with single valour stay
The adverse troops, and hold them all at bay.
Each thinks his person represents the whole,
And with that thought does multiply his soul;
Believes himself an army; there's one man,
As easily conquered; and believing, can
With heart of bees so full and head of mites,
That each, though duelling, a battle fights.
So once Orlando, famous in romance,

Broached whole brigades like larks upon his lance.
But strength at last still under number bows,
And the faint sweat trickled down Temple's brows;
Even iron Strangways chafing yet gave back,
Spent with fatigue, to breathe awhile tobac.
When marching in, a seasonable recruit
Of citizens and merchants held dispute,
And charging all their pikes, a sullen band
Of Presbyterian Switzers made a stand.

Nor could all these the field have long maintained
But for the unknown reserve that still remained;
A gross of English gentry, nobly born,
Of clear estates, and to no faction sworn,
Dear lovers of their King, and death to meet
For country's cause, that glorious think and sweet;
To speak not forward, but in action brave,
In giving generous, but in council grave;
Candidly credulous for once, nay twice;
But sure the devil cannot cheat them thrice.
The van in battle, though retiring, falls
Without disorder in their intervals,
Then closing all, in equal front, fall on,
Led by great Garroway, and great Littleton.
Lee equal to obey, or to command,
Adjutant-general was still at hand.
The marshal standard, Sands displaying, shows
St Dunstan in it tweaking Satan's nose.
See sudden chance of war, to paint or write,
Is longer work, and harder than to fight:
At the first charge the enemy give out,
And the excise receives a total rout.

Broken in courage, yet the men the same,
Resolve henceforth upon their other game:
Where force had failed, with stratagem to play,
And what haste lost, recover by delay.
St Albans straight is sent to, to forbear,
Lest the sure peace (forsooth) too soon appear.
The seamen's clamours to three ends they use,
To cheat they pay, feign want, the House accuse.
Each day they bring the tale, and that too true,

How strong the Dutch their equipage renew;
Meantime through all the yards their orders run,
To lay the ships up, cease the keels begun.
The timber rots, the useless axe does rust;
The unpractised saw lies buried in its dust;
The busy hammer sleeps, the ropes untwine;
The store and wages all are mine and thine;
Along the coasts and harbours they take care
That money lacks, nor forts be in repair.
Long thus they could against the House conspire,
Load them with envy, and with sitting tire;
And the loved King, that's never yet denied,
Is brought to beg in public, and to chide:
But when this failed, and months enough were spent,
They with the first day's proffer seem content;
And to land-tax from the excise turn round,
Bought off with eighteen hundred thousand pound.
Thus like fair thieves, the Commons' purse they share,
But all the members' lives consulting spare.
    Blither than hare that hath escaped the hounds,
The House prorogued, the Chancellor rebounds.
Not so decrepit Æson, hashed and stewed
With magic herbs, rose from the pot renewed,
And with fresh age felt his glad limbs unite;
His gout (yet still he cursed) had left him quite.
What frosts to fruits, what arsenic to the rat,
What to fair Denham mortal chocolate,
What an account to Carteret, that and more,
A parliament is to the chancellor.
So the sad tree shrinks from the morning's eye,
But blooms all night and shoots its branches high;
So at the sun's recess, again returns
The comet dread, and earth and heaven burns.
    Now Mordaunt may within his castle tower
Imprison parents, and their child deflower.
    The Irish herd is now let loose, and comes
By millions over, not by hecatombs;
And, now, now the Canary patent may
Be broached again for the great holy-day.
See how he reigns in his new palace culminant,

And sits in state divine like Jove the fulminant.
First Buckingham that durst 'gainst him rebel,
Blasted with lightning, struck with thunder fell;
Next the twelve commons are condemned to groan,
And roll in vain at Sisyphus's stone.
But still he cared, whilst in revenge he braved,
That peace secured, and money might be saved.
Gain and revenge, revenge and gain, are sweet;
United most, when most by turns they meet.
France had St Albans promised (so they sing),
St Albans promised him, and he the King.
The Count forthwith is ordered all to close,
To play for Flanders, and the stake to lose;
While chained together, two ambassadors
Like slaves shall beg for peace at Holland's doors.
This done, among his Cyclops he retires
To forge new thunder, and inspect their fires.

    The Court, as once of war, now fond of peace,
All to new sports their wonted fears release.
From Greenwich (where intelligence they hold)
Comes news of pastime martial and old.
A punishment invented first to awe
Masculine wives transgressing nature's law;
Where when the brawny female disobeys,
And beats the husband, till for peace he prays,
No concerned jury damage for him finds,
Nor partial justice her behaviour binds;
But the just street does the next house invade,
Mounting the neighbour couple on lean jade.
The distaff knocks, the grains from kettle fly,
And boys and girls in troops run hooting by.
Prudent antiquity! that knew by shame,
Better than law, domestic broils to tame;
And taught the youth by spectacle innocent:
So thou and I, dear Painter, represent
In quick effigy, others' faults; and feign,
By making them ridiculous, to restrain;
With homely sight they chose thus to relax
The joys of state for the new peace and tax.
So Holland with us had the mastery tried,

And our next neighbours, France and Flanders, ride.
    But a fresh news the great designment nips
Off, at the isle of Candy, Dutch and ships;
Bab May and Arlington did wisely scoff,
And thought all safe if they were so far off.
Modern geographers! 'twas there they thought,
Where Venice twenty years the Turks had fought,
(While the first year the navy is but shown,
The next divided, and the third we've none.)
They by the name mistook it for that isle,
Where pilgrim Palmer travelled in exile,
With the bull's horn to measure his own head,
And on Pasiphae's tomb to drop a bead.
But Morice learned demonstrates by the post,
This isle of Candy was on Essex coast.
    Fresh messengers still the sad news assure,
More timorous now we are than first secure.
False terrors our believing fears devise,
And the French army one from Calais spies.
Bennet and May, and those of shorter reach,
Change all for guineas, and a crown for each;
But wiser men, and well foreseen in chance,
In Holland theirs had lodged before, and France;
Whitehall's unsafe, the Court all meditates
To fly to Windsor, and mure up the gates.
Each doth the other blame, and all distrust,
But Mordaunt new obliged would sure be just.
Not such a fatal stupefaction reigned
At London's flames, nor so the Court complained.
The Bludworth Chancellor gives (then does recall)
Orders, amazed; at last gives none at all.
    St Albans writ too, that he may bewail
To Monsieur Lewis, and tell coward tale,
How that the Hollanders do make a noise,
Threaten to beat us, and are naughty boys.
Now Doleman 's disobedient, and they still
Uncivil, his unkindness would us kill:
Tell him our ships unrigged, our forts unmanned,
Our money spent, else 'twere at his command;
Summon him therefore of his word, and prove

To move him out of pity, if not love;
Pray him to make De Witt and Ruyter cease,
And whip the Dutch unless they'll hold their peace.
   But Lewis was of memory but dull,
And to St Albans too undutiful;
Nor word nor near relation did revere,
But asked him bluntly for his character.
The gravelled Count did with this answer faint
(His character was that which thou didst paint),
And so enforced like enemy or spy,
Trusses his baggage, and the camp does fly:
Yet Lewis writes, and lest our hearts should break,
Condoles us morally out of Senec.
   Two letters next unto Breda are sent,
In cipher one to Harry Excellent.
The first entrusts (our verse that name abhors)
Plenipotentiary ambassadors
To prove by Scripture, treaty does imply
Cessation, as the look adultery;
And that by law of arms, in martial strife,
Who yields his sword, has title to his life.
Presbyter Holles the first point should clear,
The second Coventry the cavalier:
But, would they not be argued back from sea,
Then to return home straight *infecta re*.
But Harry's ordered, if they won't recall
Their fleet, to threaten, – we will give them all.
The Dutch are then in proclamation shent,
For sin against the eleventh commandment.
Hyde's flippant style there pleasantly curvets,
Still his sharp wit on states and princes whets:
So Spain could not escape his laughter's spleen,
None but himself must choose the king a queen.
But when he came the odious clause to pen,
That summons up the Parliament again,
His writing-master many times he banned,
And wished himself the gout to seize his hand.
Never old lecher more repugnant felt,
Consenting for his rupture to be gelt.
But still in hope he solaced, ere they come

To work the peace, and so to send them home;
Or in their hasty call to find a flaw,
Their acts to vitiate, and them overawe:
But more relied upon this Dutch pretence,
To raise a two-edged army for 's defence.
    First then he marched our whole militia's force,
(As if, alas! we ships, or Dutch had horse;)
Then from the usual commonplace he blames
These, and in standing armies' praise declaims;
And the wise Court, that always loved it dear,
Now thinks all but too little for their fear.
Hyde stamps, and straight upon the ground the swarms
Of current myrmidons appear in arms:
    And for their pay he writes as from the King,
With that cursed quill plucked from a vulture's wing,
Of the whole nation now to ask a loan;
The eighteen hundred thousand pounds are gone.
This done, he pens a proclamation stout
In rescue of the bankers banquerout,
His minion imps, which in his secret part
Lie nuzzling at the sacramental wart,
Horse-leeches sucking at the hæmorrhoid vein;
He sucks the King, they him, he them again.
The kingdom's farm he lets to them bid least,
(Greater the bribe) and that's at interest.
Here men induced by safety, gain, and ease,
Their money lodge, confiscate when he please;
These can at need, at instant with a scrip,
(This liked him best) his cash beyond sea whip.
When Dutch invade, and Parliament prepare,
How can he engines so convenient spare?
Let no man touch them, or demand his own,
Pain of displeasure of great Clarendon.
    The state-affairs thus marshalled, for the rest,
Monck in his shirt against the Dutch is pressed.
Often, dear Painter, have I sat and mused
Why he should be on all adventures used;
Do they for nothing ill, like ashen wood,
Or think him, like herb-john, for nothing good?
Whether his valour they so much admire,

Or that for cowardice they all retire,
As Heaven in storms they call, in gusts of state
On Monck and Parliament, – yet both do hate.
All causes sure concur, but most they think
Under Herculean labours he may sink.
Soon then the independent troops would close,
And Hyde's last project of his place dispose.

   Ruyter, the while, that had our ocean curbed,
Sailed now amongst our rivers undisturbed;
Surveyed their crystal streams and banks so green,
And beauties ere this never naked seen:
Through the vain sedge the bashful nymphs he eyed,
Bosoms, and all which from themselves they hide.
The sun much brighter, and the sky more clear,
He finds, the air and all things sweeter here;
The sudden change, and such a tempting sight,
Swells his old veins with fresh blood, fresh delight;
Like amorous victors he begins to shave,
And his new face looks in the English wave;
His sporting navy all about him swim,
And witness their complacence in their trim;
Their streaming silks play through the weather fair,
And with inveigling colours court the air;
While the red flags breathe on their topmasts high
Terror and war, but want an enemy.
Among the shrouds the seamen sit and sing,
And wanton boys on every rope do cling;
Old Neptune springs the tides, and waters lent
(The gods themselves do help the provident),
And where the deep keel on the shallow cleaves,
With trident's lever and great shoulder heaves;
Æolus their sails inspires with eastern wind,
Puffs them along, and breathes upon them kind;
With pearly shell the Tritons all the while
Sound the sea-march, and guide to Sheppy isle.

   So have I seen in April's bud arise
A fleet of clouds sailing along the skies;
The liquid region with their squadrons filled,
Their airy sterns the sun behind doth gild,
And gentle gales them steer, and Heaven drives,

When all on sudden their calm bosom rives,
With thunder and lightning from each armèd cloud;
Shepherds themselves in vain in bushes shroud:
So up the stream the Belgic navy glides,
And at Sheerness unloads its stormy sides.

Spragge there, though practised in the sea-command,
With panting heart lay like a fish on land,
And quickly judged the fort was not tenable,
Which if a house, yet were not tenantable;
No man can sit there safe, the cannon pours
Thorough the walls untight, and bullets' showers.
The neighbourhood ill, and an unwholesome seat,
He at the first salute resolves retreat;
And swore that he would never more dwell there,
Until the city put it in repair;
So he in front, his garrison in rear,
Marched straight to Chatham to increase their fear.

There our sick ships unrigged in summer lay,
Like moulting fowl, a weak and easy prey,
For whose strong bulk earth scarce could timber find,
The ocean water, or the heavens wind;
Those oaken giants of ancient race,
That ruled all seas, and did our channel grace;
The conscious stag, though once the forest's dread,
Flies to the wood, and hides his armless head.
Ruyter forthwith a squadron does untack;
They sail securely through the river's track.
An English pilot too (O, shame! O, sin!)
Cheated of 's pay, was he that showed them in.

Our wretched ships within their fate attend,
And all our hopes now on frail chain depend,
(Engine so slight to guard us from the sea,
It fitter seemed to captivate a flea;)
A skipper rude shocks it without respect,
Filling his sails more force to re-collect;
Th' English from shore the iron deaf invoke
For its last aid: hold, chain, or we are broke!
But with her sailing weight the Holland keel,
Snapping the brittle links, does thorough reel,
And to the rest the opening passage show.

Monck from the bank that dismal sight does view:
Our feathered gallants, who came down that day
To be spectators safe of the new play,
Leave him alone when first they hear the gun,
(Cornbury the fleetest), and to London run.
　　Our seamen, whom no danger's shape could fright,
Unpaid, refuse to mount their ships for spite;
On to their fellows swim on board the Dutch,
Who show the tempting metal in their clutch.
Oft had he sent, of Duncombe and of Legge,
Cannon and powder, but in vain, to beg;
And Upnor Castle's ill-deserted wall,
Now needful does for ammunition call.
He finds, where'er he succour might expect,
Confusion, folly, treachery, fear, neglect.
　　But when the Royal Charles (what rage! what grief!)
He saw seized, and could give her no relief;
That sacred keel that had, as he, restored
Its exiled sovereign on its happy board,
And thence the British Admiral became,
Crowned for that merit with his master's name;
That pleasure-boat of war, in whose dear side
Secure, so oft he had this foe defied,
Now a cheap spoil, and the mean victor's slave,
Taught the Dutch colours from its top to wave;
Of former glories the reproachful thought,
With present shame compared, his mind distraught.
　　Such from Euphrates' bank, a tigress fell
After her robbers for her whelps doth yell,
But sees enraged the river flow between,
Frustrate revenge, and love by loss more keen;
At her own breast her useless claws does arm,
She tears herself, since him she cannot harm.
　　The guards, placed for the chain's and fleet's defence,
Long since were fled on many a feigned pretence.
　　Daniel had there adventured, man of might;
Sweet Painter, draw his picture while I write.
Paint him of person tall, and big of bone,
Large limbs like ox, not to be killed but shown.
Scarce can burnt ivory feign a hair so black,

Or face so red thine ochre and thy lac;
Mix a vain terror in his martial look,
And all those lines by which men are mistook.
But when by shame constrained to go on board,
He heard how the wild cannon nearer roared,
And saw himself confined like sheep in pen,
Daniel then thought he was in lion's den.
But when the frightful fire-ships he saw,
Pregnant with sulphur, nearer to him draw,
Captain, Lieutenant, Ensign, all make haste,
Ere in the fiery furnace they be cast;
Three children tall, unsinged, away they row,
Like Shadrach, Meshech, and Abednego.
Each doleful day still with fresh loss returns,
The Loyal London now a third time burns;
And the true Royal Oak, and Royal James,
Allied in fate, increase with theirs her flames.
Of all our navy none should now survive,
But that the ships themselves were taught to dive,
And the kind river in its creek them hides
Freighting their piercèd keels with oozy tides;
Up to the Bridge contagious terror struck,
The Tower itself with the near danger shook;
And were not Ruyter's maw with ravage cloyed,
Even London's ashes had been then destroyed.
Officious fear, however, to prevent
Our loss, does so much more our loss augment.
The Dutch had robbed those jewels of the Crown;
Our merchant-men, lest they should burn, we drown;
So when the fire did not enough devour,
The houses were demolished near the Tower.
Those ships that yearly from their teeming hole
Unloaded here the birth of either pole,
Fur from the north, and silver from the west,
From the south perfumes, spices from the east,
From Gambo gold, and from the Ganges gems,
Take a short voyage underneath the Thames,
Once a deep river, now with timber floored,
And shrunk, less navigable, to a ford.
   Now nothing more at Chatham 's left to burn,

The Holland squadron leisurely return;
And spite of Rupert's and of Albermarle's,
To Ruyter's triumph led the captive Charles.
The pleasing sight he often does prolong,
Her mast erect, tough cordage, timber strong,
Her moving shape, all these he doth survey,
And all admires, but most his easy prey.
The seamen search her all within, without;
Viewing her strength, they yet their conquest doubt;
Then with rude shouts, secure, the air they vex,
With gamesome joy insulting on her decks.
Such the feared Hebrew captive, blinded, shorn,
Was led about in sport the public scorn.

 Black day, accursed! on thee let no man hail
Out of the port, or dare to hoist a sail,
Or row a boat in thy unlucky hour!
Thee, the year's monster, let thy dam devour,
And constant Time, to keep his course yet right,
Fill up thy space with a redoubled night.
When agèd Thames was bound with fetters base,
And Medway chaste ravished before his face,
And their dear offspring murdered in their sight,
Thou and thy fellows saw the odious light.
Sad change, since first that happy pair was wed,
With all the rivers graced their nuptial bed;
And father Neptune promised to resign
His empire old to their immortal line;
Now with vain grief their vainer hopes they rue,
Themselves dishonoured, and the gods untrue;
And to each other, helpless couple, moan,
As the sad tortoise for the sea does groan:
But most they for their darling Charles complain,
And were it burned, yet less would be their pain.
To see that fatal pledge of sea-command,
Now in the ravisher De Ruyter's hand,
The Thames roared, swooning Medway turned her tide,
And were they mortal, both for grief had died.

 The Court in fathering yet itself doth please,
(And female Stewart there rules the four seas.)
But fate does still accumulate our woes,

And Richmond her commands, as Ruyter those.
   After this loss, to relish discontent,
Some one must be accused by Parliament.
All our miscarriages on Pett must fall,
His name alone seems fit to answer all.
Whose counsel first did this mad war beget?
Who all commands sold through the navy? Pett.
Who would not follow when the Dutch were beat?
Who treated out the time at Bergen? Pett.
Who the Dutch fleet with storms disabled met?
And, rifling prizes, them neglected? Pett.
Who with false news prevented the Gazette?
The fleet divided? writ for Rupert? Pett.
Who all our seamen cheated of their debt,
And all our prizes who did swallow? Pett.
Who did advise no navy out to set?
And who the forts left unpreparèd? Pett.
Who to supply with powder did forget
Languard, Sheerness, Gravesend, and Upnor? Pett.
Who all our ships exposed in Chatham net?
Who should it be but the fanatic Pett?
Pett, the sea-architect in making ships,
Was the first cause of all these naval slips;
Had he not built, none of these faults had been;
If no creation, there had been no sin;
But his great crime, one boat away he sent,
That lost our fleet and did our flight prevent.
Then, that reward might in its turn take place,
And march with punishment in equal pace,
Southampton dead, much of the treasure's care,
And place in council, fell to Duncombe's share.
All men admired he to that pitch could fly:
Powder ne'er blew man up so soon, so high;
But sure his late good husbandry in petre
Showed him to manage the Exchequer meeter;
And who the forts would not vouchsafe a corn,
To lavish the King's money more would scorn;
Who hath no chimneys, to give all, is best,
And ablest speaker, who of law hath least;
Who less estate, for treasurer most fit,

And for a chancellor he that has least wit;
But the true cause was, that in 's brother May,
The Exchequer might the privy-purse obey.
    And now draws near the Parliament's return;
Hyde and the Court again begin to mourn;
Frequent in council, earnest in debate,
All arts they try how to prolong its date.
Grave Primate Sheldon (much in preaching there)
Blames the last session, and this more does fear:
With Boynton or with Middleton 'twere sweet,
But with a Parliament abhors to meet;
And thinks 'twill ne'er be well within this nation,
Till it be governed by a Convocation.
    But in the Thames' mouth still De Ruyter laid;
The peace not sure, new army must be paid.
Hyde saith he hourly waits for a despatch;
Harry came post just as he showed his watch.
All do agree the articles were clear,
The Holland fleet and Parliament so near,
Yet Harry must job back and all mature,
Binding, ere the Houses meet, the treaty sure;
And 'twixt neccssity and spite, till then
Let them come up, so to go down again.
Up ambles country justice on his pad,
And vest bespeaks, to be more seemly clad.
Plain gentlemen are in stage-coach o'erthrown,
And deputy-lieutenants in their own;
The portly burgess, through the weather hot,
Does for his corporation sweat and trot;
And all with sun and choler come adust,
And threaten Hyde to raise a greater dust.
    But fresh, as from the mint, the courtiers fine
Salute them, smiling at their vain design;
And Turner gay up to his perch doth march,
With face new bleached, smoothèd, and stiff with starch;
Tells them he at Whitehall had took a turn,
And for three days thence moves them to adjourn.
Not so, quoth Tomkins, and straight drew his tongue,
Trusty as steel that always ready hung;
And so proceeding in his motion warm,

Th' army soon raised, he doth as soon disarm.
True Trojan! whilst this town can girls afford,
And long as cider lasts in Hereford,
The girls shall always kiss thee, though grown old,
And in eternal healths thy name be trolled.

   Meanwhile the certain news of peace arrives
At Court, and so reprieves their guilty lives.

   Hyde orders Turner that he should come late,
Lest some new Tomkins spring a fresh debate;
The King, that early raised was from his rest,
Expects, as at a play, till Turner's dressed;
At last, together Eaton came and he,
No dial more could with the sun agree;
The Speaker, summoned to the Lords, repairs,
Nor gave the Commons leave to say their prayers,
But like his prisoners to the bar them led,
Where mute they stand to hear their sentence read:
Trembling with joy and fear, Hyde them prorogues,
And had almost mistook, and called them rogues.

   Dear Painter, draw this Speaker to the foot:
Where pencil cannot, there my pen shall do 't;
That may his body, this his mind explain;
Paint him in golden gown with mace's train;
Bright hair, fair face, obscure and dull of head,
Like knife with ivory haft, and edge of lead:
At prayers his eyes turn up the pious white,
But all the while his private bill's in sight:
In chair he smoking sits like master cook,
And a poll-bill does like his apron look.
Well was he skilled to season any question,
And make a sauce fit for Whitehall's digestion,
Whence every day, the palate more to tickle,
Court-mushrooms ready are sent in to pickle.
When grievance urged, he swells like squatted toad,
Frisks like a frog to croak a tax's load:
His patient piss he could hold longer than
An urinal, and sit like any hen;
At table jolly as a country host,
And soaks his sack with Norfolk like a toast;
At night than chanticleer more brisk and hot,

And sergeant's wife serves him for partelot.
    Paint last the King, and a dead shade of night,
Only dispersed by a weak taper's light,
And those bright gleams that dart along and glare
From his clear eyes, (yet these too dart with care;)
There, as in the calm horror all alone,
He wakes and muses of the uneasy throne,
Raise up a sudden shape with virgin's face,
Though ill agree her posture, hour or place;
Naked as born, and her round arms behind,
With her own tresses interwove and twined;
Her mouth locked up, a blind before her eyes,
Yet from beneath her veil her blushes rise;
And silent tears her secret anguish speak,
Her heart throbs, and with very shame would break.
The object strange in him no terror moved,
He wondered first, then pitied, then he loved;
And with kind hand does the coy vision press,
Whose beauty greater seemed by her distress:
But soon shrunk back, chilled with a touch so cold,
And the airy picture vanished from his hold.
In his deep thoughts the wonder did increase,
And he divined 'twas England, or the peace.
    Express him startling next, with listening ear,
As one that some unusual noise doth hear;
With cannons, trumpets, drums, his door surround,
But let some other Painter draw the sound.
Thrice he did rise, thrice the vain tumult fled,
But again thunders when he lies in bed.
His mind secure does the vain stroke repeat,
And finds the drums Lewis's march did beat.
    Shake then the room, and all his curtains tear,
And with blue streaks infect the taper clear,
While the pale ghost his eyes doth fixed admire
Of grandsire Harry, and of Charles his sire.
Harry sits down, and in his open side
The grisly wound reveals of which he died;
And ghastly Charles, turning his collar low,
The purple thread about his neck does show;
Then whispering to his son in words unheard,

Through the locked door both of them disappeared.
The wondrous night the pensive King revolves,
And rising straight, on Hyde's disgrace resolves.
    At his first step he Castlemaine does find,
Bennet and Coventry as 'twas designed;
And they not knowing, the same thing propose
Which his hid mind did in its depths inclose.
Through their feigned speech their secret hearts he knew,
To her own husband Castlemaine untrue;
False to his master Bristol, Arlington;
And Coventry falser than any one,
Who to the brother, brother would betray;
Nor therefore trusts himself to such as they.
His father's ghost too whispered him one note,
That who does cut his purse will cut his throat;
But in wise anger he their crimes forbears,
As thieves reprieved from executioners;
While Hyde, provoked, his foaming tusk does whet,
To prove them traitors, and himself the Pett.
    Painter, adieu. How well our arts agree!
Poetic picture, painted poetry!
But this great work is for our monarch fit,
And henceforth Charles only to Charles shall sit;
His master-hand the ancients shall outdo,
Himself the Painter, and the Poet too.

TO THE KING

So his bold tube man to the sun applied,
And spots unknown in the bright star descried;
Showed they obscure him, while too near they please,
And seem his courtiers, are but his disease;
Through optic trunk the planet seemed to hear,
And hurls them off e'er since in his career.
    And you, great Sir, that with him empire share,
Sun of our world, as he the Charles is there,
Blame not the Muse that brought those spots to sight,
Which, in your splendour hid, corrode your light;
(Kings in the country oft have gone astray,

Nor of a peasant scorned to learn the way.)
Would she the unattended throne reduce,
Banishing love, trust, ornament, and use?
Better it were to live in cloister's lock,
Or in fair fields to rule the easy flock:
She blames them only who the Court restrain,
And where all England serves, themselves would reign.

Bold and accursed are they who all this while
Have strove to isle the monarch from this isle,
And to improve themselves by false pretence,
About the common prince have raised a fence;
The kingdom from the crown distinct would see,
And peel the bark to burn at last the tree.
As Ceres corn, and Flora is the spring,
Bacchus is wine, the Country is the King.

Not so does rust insinuating wear,
Nor powder so the vaulted bastion tear,
Nor earthquakes so an hollow isle o'erwhelm,
As scratching courtiers undermine a realm,
And through the palace's foundations bore,
Burrowing themselves to hoard their guilty store.
The smallest vermin make the greatest waste,
And a poor warren once a city rased.
But they who born to virtue and to wealth,
Nor guilt to flattery binds, nor want to stealth;
Whose generous conscience, and whose courage high,
Does with clear counsels their large souls supply;
Who serve the King with their estates and care,
And as in love on parliaments can stare;
Where few the number, choice is there less hard;
Give us this Court, and rule without a guard.

Clarendon's House-warming

I

When Clarendon had discerned beforehand
   (As the cause can easily foretell the effect)
At once three deluges threatening our land,
    'Twas the season, he thought, to turn architect.

II

Us Mars, and Apollo, and Vulcan consume;
   While he, the betrayer of England and Flanders,
Like the kingfisher chooseth to build in the broom,
    And nestles in flames like the salamanders.

III

But observing that mortals run often behind
   (So unreasonable are the rates that they buy at),
His omnipotence therefore much rather designed,
    How he might create a house with a fiat.

IV

He had read of Rhodope, a lady of Thrace,
   Who was digged up so often ere she did marry;
And wished that his daughter had had as much grace,
    To erect him a pyramid out of her quarry.

V

But then recollecting how the harper Amphion
   Made Thebes dance aloft while he fiddled and sung,
He thought, as an instrument he was most free on,
    To build with the Jew's-trump of his own tongue.

VI

Yet a precedent fitter in Virgil he found,
   Of African Poultney, and Tyrian Dide;
That he begged for a palace so much of his ground,
    As might carry the measure and name of a Hyde.

VII

Thus daily his gouty inventions him pained,
　　And all for to save the expenses of brickbat;
That engine so fatal which Denham had brained,
　　And too much resembled his wife's chocolate.

VIII

But while these devices he all doth compare,
　　None solid enough seemed for his strong castor;
He himself would not dwell in a castle of air,
　　Though he had built full many a one for his master.

IX

Already he had got all our money and cattle,
　　To buy us for slaves, and purchase our lands;
What Joseph by famine, he wrought by sea battle;
　　Nay, scarce the priest's portion could 'scape from his
　　　hands.

X

And hence like Pharaoh that Israel pressed
　　To make mortar and brick, yet allowed 'em no straw,
He cared not though Egypt's ten plagues us distressed,
　　So he could to build but make policy law.

XI

The Scotch forts and Dunkirk, but that they were sold,
　　He would have demolished to raise up his walls;
Nay, e'en from Tangier have sent back for the mould,
　　But that he had nearer the stones of St Paul's.

XII

His woods would come in at the easier rate,
　　So long as the yards had a deal or a spar:
His friend in the navy would not be ingrate,
　　To grudge him some timber, who framed him the war.

XIII

To proceed in the model, he called in his Allens,
    The two Allens, when jovial, who ply him with gallons;
The two Allens who served his blind justice for balance,
    The two Allens who served his injustice for talons.

XIV

They approve it thus far, and said it was fine;
    Yet his lordship to finish it would be unable,
Unless all abroad he divulged the design,
    For his house then would grow like a vegetable.

XV

His rent would no more in arrear run to Wor'ster;
    He should dwell more noble and cheap too at home,
While into a fabric the presents would muster;
    As by hook and by crook the world clustered of atom.

XVI

He liked the advice and then soon it assayed,
    And presents crowd headlong to give good example,
So the bribes overlaid her that Rome once betrayed;
    The tribes ne'er contributed so to the Temple.

XVII

Straight judges, priests, bishops, true sons of the seal,
    Sinners, governors, farmers, bankers, patentees,
Bring in the whole mite of a year at a meal,
    As the Cheddar club's dairy to the incorporate cheese.

XVIII

Bulteale's, Beaken's, Morley's, Wren's fingers with telling
    Were shrivelled, and Clutterbuck's, Eager's, and Kipps';
Since the act of oblivion was never such selling,
    As at this benevolence out of the snips.

XIX

'Twas then that the chimney-contractors he smoked,
   Nor would take his beloved canary in kind:
But he swore that the patent should ne'er be revoked,
   No, would the whole parliament kiss him behind.

XX

Like Jove under Ætna o'erwhelming the giant,
   For foundation the Bristol sunk in the earth's bowel;
And St John must now for the leads be compliant,
   Or his right hand shall be cut off with a trowel.

XXI

For surveying the building, 'twas Prat did the feat;
   But for the expense he relied on Worstenholme,
Who sat heretofore at the King's receipt,
   But received now and paid the Chancellor's custom.

XXII

By subsidies thus both cleric and laic,
   And with matter profane cemented with holy;
He finished at last his palace mosaic,
   By a model more excellent than Lesly's folly.

XXIII

And upon the terrace to consummate all,
   A lantern like Faux's surveys the burnt town,
And shows on the top by the regal gilt ball,
   Where you are to expect the sceptre and crown.

XXIV

Fond city, its rubbish and ruins that builds,
   Like vain chemists, a flower from its ashes returning,
Your metropolis house is in St James's fields,
   And till there you remove, you shall never leave burning.

XXV

This temple of war and of peace is the shrine,
    Where this idol of state sits adored and accursed;
To handsel his altar and nostrils divine,
    Great Buckingham's sacrifice must be the first.

XXVI

Now some (as all builders must censure abide)
    Throw dust in its front and blame situation:
And others as much reprehend his back-side,
    As too narrow by far for his expatiation;

XXVII

But do not consider how in process of times,
    That for namesake he may with Hyde Park it enlarge,
And with that convenience he soon, for his crimes,
    At Tyburn may land and spare the Tower barge.

XXVIII

Or rather how wisely his stall was built near,
    Lest with driving too far his tallow impair;
When, like the good ox, for public good cheer,
    He comes to be roasted next St James's fair.

Upon His House

Here lie the sacred bones
Of Paul beguilèd of his stones:
Here lie golden briberies,
The price of ruined families;
The cavalier's debenture wall,
Fixed on an eccentric basis;
Here's Dunkirk Town and Tangier Hall,
The Queen's marriage and all,
The Dutchman's *templum pacis*.

Epigram upon His Grandchildren

Kendal is dead, and Cambridge riding post;
What fitter sacrifice for Denham's ghost?

Farther Instructions to a Painter

Painter, once more thy pencil reassume,
And draw me, in one scene, London and Rome:
Here holy Charles, there good Aurelius sat,
Weeping to see their sons degenerate;
His Romans taking up the teemer's trade,
The Britons jigging it in masquerade;
Whilst the brave youths, tired with the toil of state,
Their weary minds and limbs to recreate,
Do to their more beloved delights repair,
One to his whore, the other to his player.
  Then change the scene, and let the next present
A landscape of our motley Parliament;
And place, hard by the bar, on the left hand,

Circean Clifford with his charming wand;
Our pig-eyed — on his — fashion,
Set by the worst attorney of our nation,
This great triumvirate that can divide
The spoils of England; and along that side
Place Falstaff's regiment of threadbare coats,
All looking this way, how to give their votes;
And of his dear reward let none despair,
For money comes when Seymour leaves the chair.
Change once again, and let the next afford
The figure of a motley council-board
At Arlington's, and round about it set
Our mighty masters in a warm debate.
Full bowls of lusty wine make them repeat,
To make the other council-board forget
That while the King of France with powerful arms
Gives all his fearful neighbours strange alarms,
We in our glorious bacchanals dispose
The humbled fate of a plebeian nose;
Which to effect, when thus it was decreed,
Draw me a champion mounted on a steed;
And after him a brave brigade of horse,
Armed at all points, ready to re-enforce
Him, in's assault upon a single man.

*

'Tis this must make O'Bryan great in story,
And add more beams to Sandy's former glory.
  Draw our Olympia next, in council set
With Cupid, S[eymou]r, and the tool of state:
Two of the first recanters of the house,
That aim at mountains, and bring forth a mouse;
Who make it, by their mean retreat, appear
Five members need not be demanded here.
These must assist her in her countermines,
To overthrow the Derby House designs;
Whilst Positive walks, like woodcock in the park,
Contriving projects with a brewer's clerk;
Thus all employ themselves, and, without pity,
Leave Temple singly to be beat in the city.

On Blood's Stealing the Crown

When daring Blood, his rent to have regained,
Upon the English diadem distrained,
He chose the cassock, surcingle, and gown,
The fittest mask for one that robs the crown:
But his lay-pity underneath prevailed,
And whilst he saved the keeper's life he failed;
With the priest's vestment had he but put on
The prelate's cruelty, the crown had gone.

A Poem on the Statue in Stocks-Market

I

As cities that to the fierce conqueror yield
Do at their own charges their citadels build;
So Sir Robert advanced the King's statue, in token
Of bankers defeated, and Lombard Street broken.

II

Some thought it a knightly and generous deed,
Obliging the city with a King and a steed;
When with honour he might from his word have gone
    back:
He that rows for a calm is absolved by a wreck.

III

But now it appears, from the first to the last,
To be all a revenge, and a malice forecast;
Upon the King's birthday to set up a thing
That shows him a monkey more like than a King.

IV

When each one that passes finds fault with the horse,
Yet all do affirm that the King is much worse;
And some by the likeness Sir Robert suspect
That he did for the King his own statue erect.

V

Thus to see him disfigured – the herb-women chide,
Who up on their panniers more gracefully ride;
And so loose in his seat – that all persons agree,
E'en Sir William Peake sits much firmer than he.

VI

But a market, as some say, doth fit the King well,
Who the Parliament too and revenue doth sell;
And others, to make the similitude hold,
Say his Majesty too is oft purchased and sold.

VII

This statue is surely more scandalous far
Than all the Dutch pictures which causèd the war;
And what the Exchequer for that took on trust
May we henceforth confiscate, for reasons more just.

VIII

But Sir Robert, to take all the scandal away,
Does the error upon the artificer lay;
And alleges the workmanship was not his own,
For he counterfeits only in gold, not in stone.

IX

But, Sir Knight of the Vine, how came't in your thought,
That when to the scaffold your liege you had brought,
With canvas and deals you e'er since do him cloud,
As if you had meant it his coffin and shroud?

X

Hath Blood [stole] him away, as his crown he conveyed?
Or is he to Clayton's gone in masquerade?
Or is he in cabal in his cabinet set?
Or have you to the Compter removed him for debt?

XI

Methinks by the equipage of this vile scene,
That to change him into a jack-pudding you mean;
Or why thus expose him to popular flouts,
As if we'd as good have a King made of clouts?

XII

Or do you his faults out of modesty veil
With three shattered planks, and the rag of a sail;
To express how his navy was shattered and torn,
The day that he was both restorèd and born?

XIII

Sure the King will ne'er think of repaying his bankers,
When loyalty now all expires with his spankers;
If the Indies and Smyrna do not him enrich,
He will hardly have left a poor rag to his breech.

XIV

But Sir Robert affirms that we do him much wrong;
'Tis the 'graver at work, to reform him, so long;
But, alas! he will never arrive at his end,
For it is such a King as no chisel can mend.

XV

But with all his errors restore us our King,
If ever you hope in December for Spring;
For though all the world cannot show such another,
Yet we'd rather have him than his bigotted brother.

An Historical Poem

Of a tall stature, and of sable hue,
Much like the son of Kish, that lofty Jew,
Twelve years complete he suffered in exile,
And kept his father's asses all the while;
At length, by wonderful impulse of fate,
The people call him home to help the state,
And, what is more, they send him money too,
And clothe him all, from head to foot, anew.
Nor did he such small favours then disdain,
Who in his thirtieth year began his reign:
In a slashed doublet then he came ashore,
And dubbed poor Palmer's wife his royal whore.
Bishops, and deans, peers, pimps, and knights, he made,
Things highly fitting for a monarch's trade!
With women, wine, and viands of delight,
His jolly vassals feast him day and night.
But the best times have ever some allay,
His younger brother died by treachery.
Bold James survives, no dangers make him flinch;
He marries Signor Falmouth's pregnant wench.
The pious mother queen, hearing her son
Was thus enamoured with a buttered bun,
And that the fleet was gone, in pomp and state,
To fetch, for Charles, the flowery Lisbon Kate,
She chants *Te Deum*, and so comes away,
To wish her hopeful issue timely joy.
Her most uxorious mate she ruled of old,
Why not with easy youngsters make as bold?
From the French Court she haughty topics brings,
Deludes their pliant nature with vain things;
Her mischief-breeding breast did so prevail,
The new-got Flemish town was set to sale;
For these, and Jermyn's sins, she founds a church,
So slips away, and leaves us in the lurch.
Now the Court-sins did every place defile,
And plagues and war fall heavy on the isle;

Pride nourished folly, folly a delight
With the Batavian Commonwealth to fight;
But the Dutch fleet fled suddenly with fear,
Death and the Duke so dreadful did appear.
The dreadful victor took his soft repose,
Scorning pursuit of such mechanic foes.

But now York's genitals grew over hot,
With Denham's and Carnegie's infected plot,
Which, with religion, so inflamed his ire,
He left the city when 'twas got on fire.
So Philip's son, inflamèd with a miss,
Burned down the palace of Persepolis.
Foiled thus by Venus, he Bellona woos,
And with the Dutch a second war renews;
But here his French-bred prowess proved in vain,
De Ruyter claps him in Solebay again.

This isle was well reformed, and gained renown,
Whilst the brave Tudors wore the imperial crown:
But since the royal race of Stuarts came,
It has recoiled to Popery and shame;
Misguided monarchs, rarely wise or just,
Tainted with pride, and with impetuous lust.

Should we the Blackheath project here relate,
Or count the various blemishes of state,
My muse would on the reader's patience grate.

The poor Priapus King, led by the nose,
Looks as a thing set up to scare the crows;
Yet, in the mimics of the spintrian sport,
Outdoes Tiberius, and his goatish Court.
In love's delights none did them e'er excel,
Not Tereus with his sister Philomel;
As they at Athens, we at Dover meet,
And gentlier far the Orleans Duchess treat.
What sad event attended on the same
We'll leave to the report of common fame.

The senate, which should headstrong princes stay,
Let loose the reins, and give the realm away
With lavish hands they constant tributes give,
And annual stipends for their guilt receive;
Corrupt with gold, they wives and daughters bring

To the black idol for an offering.
All but religious cheats might justly swear,
He true vicegerent to old Moloch were.
    Priests were the first deluders of mankind,
Who with vain faith made all their reason blind;
Not Lucifer himself more proud than they,
And yet persuade the world they must obey;
'Gainst avarice and luxury complain,
And practise all the vices they arraign.
Riches and honour they from laymen reap,
And with dull crambo feed the silly sheep.
As Killigrew buffoons his master, they
Droll on their god, but a much duller way.
With hocus-pocus, and their heavenly sleight,
They gain on tender consciences at night.
Whoever has an over-zealous wife
Becomes the priest's Amphitryo during life.
Who would such men Heaven's messengers believe,
Who from the sacred pulpit dare deceive?
Baal's wretched curates legerdemained it so,
And never durst their tricks above-board show.
    When our first parents Paradise did grace,
The serpent was the prelate of the place;
Fond Eve did, for this subtle tempter's sake,
From the forbidden tree the pippin take;
His God and Lord this preacher did betray,
To have the weaker vessel made his prey.
Since death and sin did human nature blot,
The chiefest blessings Adam's chaplain got.
    Thrice wretched they, who nature's laws detest,
To trace the ways fantastic of a priest,
Till native reason's basely forced to yield,
And hosts of upstart errors gain the field.
    My muse presumed a little to digress,
And touch their holy function with my verse.
Now to the state again she tends direct,
And does on giant Lauderdale reflect.
This haughty monster, with his ugly claws,
First tempered poison to destroy our laws;
Declares the council's edicts are beyond

The most authentic statutes of the land;
Sets up in Scotland *à la mode de* France;
Taxes, excise, and armies does advance.
This Saracen his country's freedom broke,
To bring upon their necks the heavier yoke;
This is the savage pimp, without dispute,
First brought his mother for a prostitute;
Of all the miscreants e'er went to hell,
This villain rampant bears away the bell.
   Now must my muse deplore the nation's fate,
Like a true lover for her dying mate.
The royal evil so malignant grows,
Nothing the dire contagion can oppose.
In our weal-public scarce one thing succeeds,
For one man's weakness a whole nation bleeds;
Ill-luck starts up, and thrives like evil weeds.
Let Cromwell's ghost smile with contempt, to see
Old England struggling under slavery.
   His meagre Highness, now he's got astride,
Does on Britannia, as on Churchill, ride.
   White-livered P— [calls] for his swift jackall
To hunt down 's prey, and hopes to master all.
   Clifford and Hyde before had lost the day;
One hanged himself, and t' other ran away.
'T was want of wit and courage made them fail,
But O[sbor]ne, and the Duke, must needs prevail.
The Duke now vaunts with Popish myrmidons;
Our fleets, our ports, our cities and our towns,
Are manned by him, or by his Holiness;
Bold Irish ruffians to his Court address.
This is the colony to plant his knaves,
From hence he picks and culls his murdering braves.
Here for an ensign, or lieutenant's place,
They'll kill a judge or justice of the peace.
At his command Mac will do any thing:
He'll burn a city, or destroy a King.
From Tiber came the advice-boat monthly home,
And brought new lessons to the Duke from Rome.
Here, with cursed precepts, and with counsels dire,
The godly cheat-king (would be) did aspire;

Heaven had him chieftain of Great Britain made,
Tells him the holy church demands his aid;
Bade him be bold, all dangers to defy,
His brother, sneaking heretic, should die;
A priest should do it, from whose sacred stroke
All England straight should fall beneath his yoke;
God did renounce him, and his cause disown,
And in his stead had placed him on his throne.
From Saul the land of promise thus was rent,
And Jesse's son placed in the government.
The Holy Scripture vindicates his cause,
And monarchs are above all human laws.

Thus said the Scarlet Whore to her gallant,
Who straight designed his brother to supplant:
Fiends of ambition here his soul possessed,
And thirst of empire calentured his breast.

Hence ruin and destruction had ensued,
And all the people been in blood imbrued,
Had not Almighty Providence drawn near,
And stopped his malice in his full career.

Be wise, ye sons of men, tempt God no more
To give you kings in 's wrath to vex you sore:
If a King's brother can such mischiefs bring,
Then how much greater mischiefs such a King.

Advice to a Painter

Spread a large canvas, Painter, to contain
The great assembly and the numerous train,
Who all about him shall in council sit,
Abjuring wisdom, and despising wit;
Hating all justice, and resolved to fight,
To rob his native country of its right.
    First draw his Highness prostrate to the south,
Adoring Rome, this label in his mouth, –
'Most holy Father! being joined in league
With Father Patrick, Darby, and with Teague,
Thrown at your sacred feet, I humbly bow,
I, and the wise associates of my vow,
A vow nor fire nor sword shall ever end,
Till all this nation to your footstool bend.
Thus armed with zeal and blessings from your hands,
I'll raise my Irish and my Popish bands,
And by a noble well-contrivèd plot,
Managed by wise Fitz-Gerrard, and by Scott,
Prove to the world I'll have Old England know
That common sense is my eternal foe.
I ne'er can fight in a more glorious cause,
Than to destroy their liberties and laws,
Their House of Commons, and their House of Lords,
Their parchment precedents, and dull records;
Shall these e'er dare to contradict my will,
And think a prince of the blood can e'er do ill?
It is our birthright to have power to kill.
Shall these men dare to think, shall these decide
The way to heaven, and who shall be my guide?
Shall these pretend to say that bread is bread,
[If we affirm it is a God indeed?]
Or there's no Purgatory for the dead?
That extreme unction is but common oil?
And not infallible the Roman soil?
I'll have these villains in our notions rest;
You and I say it, therefore it 's the best.'
        Next, Painter, draw his Mordaunt by his side,

Conveying his religion and his bride:
He, who long since abjured the royal line,
Does now in Popery with his master join.
    Then draw the princess with her golden locks,
Hastening to be envenomed with the p—,
And in her youthful veins receive a wound,
Which sent N— H— before her under ground;
The wound of which the tainted C— fades,
Preserved in store for the next set of maids.
    Poor princess, born under some sullen star,
To find this welcome when you came so far!
Better some jealous neighbour of your own
Had called you to some sound, though petty throne;
Where, 'twixt a wholesome husband and a page,
You might have lingered out a lazy age,
Than on dull hopes of being here a Queen,
Die before twenty, rot before fifteen.
    Now, Painter, show us in the blackest dye,
The counsellors of all this villany.
    Clifford, who first appeared in humble guise,
Was thought so meek, so modest, and so wise;
But when he came to act upon the stage,
He proved the mad Cethegus of our age.
He and the Duke had each too great a mind
To be by justice or by law confined:
Their boiling heads can hear no other sounds,
Than fleets and armies, battles, blood, and wounds:
And to destroy our liberty they hope,
By Irish fools, and an old doting Pope.
    [Next, Talbot must by his great master stand,
Laden with folly, flesh, and ill-got land;
He 's of a size indeed to fill a porch,
But ne'er can make a pillar of the church.
His sword is all his argument, not his book;
Although no scholar, he can act the cook,
And will cut throats again, if he be paid;
In the Irish shambles he first learned the trade.]
    Then, Painter, show thy skill, and in fit place
Let 's see the nuncio Arundel's sweet face;
Let the beholders by thy art espy

His sense and soul, as squinting as his eye.
   Let Bellasis' autumnal face be seen,
Rich with the spoils of a poor Algerine,
Who, trusting in him, was by him betrayed;
And so should we, were his advice obeyed.
The hero once got honour by the sword;
He got his wealth by breaking of his word;
He now hath got his daughter great with child,
And pimps to have his family defiled.
   Next, Painter, draw the rabble of the plot;
Jermyn, Fitz-Gerald, Loftus, Porter, Scott:
These are fit heads indeed to turn a state,
And change the order of a nation's fate;
Ten thousand such as these can ne'er control
The smallest atom of an English soul.
   Old England on its strong foundation stands,
Defying all their heads and all their hands;
Its steady basis never could be shook,
When wiser heads its ruin undertook;
And can her guardian angel let her stoop
At last to fools, to madmen, and the Pope?
No, Painter, no! close up thy piece, and see
This crowd of traitors hang in effigy.

TO THE KING

Great Charles, who full of mercy might'st command
In peace and pleasure this thy native land,
At last take pity on thy tottering throne,
Shook by the faults of others, not thy own;
Let not thy life and crown together end,
Destroyed by a false brother, and false friend.
Observe the danger that appears so near,
And all your subjects do each minute fear;
A drop of poison, or a Popish knife,
Ends all the joys of England with your life.
Brothers, 'tis true, should be by nature kind;
But to a zealous and ambitious mind,
Bribed by a crown on earth, and one above,

There's no more friendship, tenderness, or love.
See in all ages what examples are
Of monarchs murdered by the impatient heir.
Hard fate of princes, who will ne'er believe,
Till the stroke's struck which they can ne'er retrieve!

Britannia and Raleigh

Britannia Ah! Raleigh, when thou didst thy breath resign
To trembling James, would I had quitted mine.
Cubs didst thou call them? Hadst thou seen this
    brood
Of earls, and dukes, and princes of the blood,
No more of Scottish race thou would'st complain,
These would be blessings in this spurious reign.
Awake, arise from thy long blest repose,
Once more with me partake of mortal woes!

Raleigh What mighty power has forced me from my rest?
Oh! mighty queen, why so untimely dressed?

Britannia Favoured by night, concealed in this disguise,
Whilst the lewd Court in drunken slumber lies,
I stole away, and never will return,
Till England knows who did her city burn;
Till cavaliers shall favourites be deemed,
And loyal sufferers by the Court esteemed;
Till Lee and Galloway shall bribes reject;
Thus Osborne's golden cheat I shall detect:
Till atheist Lauderdale shall leave this land,
And Commons' votes shall cut-nose guards disband:
Till Kate a happy mother shall become,
Till Charles loves Parliaments, and James hates Rome.

Raleigh What fatal crimes make you for ever fly
Your once loved Court, and martyr's progeny?

Britannia A colony of French possess the Court;
Pimps, priests, buffoons, in privy-chamber sport.

Such slimy monsters ne'er approached a throne
Since Pharaoh's days, nor so defiled a crown.
In sacred ear tyrannic arts they croak,
Pervert his mind, and good intentions choke;
Tell him of golden Indies, fairy lands,
Leviathan, and absolute commands.
Thus, fairy-like, the King they steal away,
And in his room a changeling Lewis lay.
How oft have I him to himself restored,
In 's left the scale, in 's right hand placed the sword?
Taught him their use, what dangers would ensue
To them who strive to separate these two?
The bloody Scottish chronicle read o'er,
Showed him how many kings, in purple gore,
Were hurled to hell, by cruel tyrant lore?

   The other day famed Spenser I did bring,
In lofty notes Tudor's blest race to sing;
How Spain's proud powers her virgin arms
    controlled,
And golden days in peaceful order rolled;
How like ripe fruit she dropped from off her throne,
Full of gray hairs, good deeds, and great renown.
As the Jessean hero did appease
Saul's stormy rage, and stopped his black disease,
So the learned bard, with artful song, suppressed
The swelling passion of his cankered breast,
And in his heart kind influences shed
Of country's love, by truth and justice bred.
Then to perform the cure so well begun,
To him I showed this glorious setting sun;
How, by her people's looks pursued from far,
She mounted on a bright celestial car,
Outshining Virgo, or the Julian star.
Whilst in Truth's mirror this good scene he spied,
Entered a dame, bedecked with spotted pride,
Fair flower-de-luce within an azure field;
Her left hand bears the ancient Gallic shield,
By her usurped; her right a bloody sword,
Inscribed Leviathan, our sovereign Lord;
Her towery front a fiery meteor bears,

An exhalation bred of blood and tears;
Around her Jove's lewd ravenous curs complain,
Pale Death, Lust, tortures, fill her pompous train;
She from the easy King Truth's mirror took,
And on the ground in spiteful fall it broke;
Then frowning thus, with proud disdain she spoke:
   'Are thread-bare virtues ornaments for kings?
Such poor pedantic toys teach underlings.
Do monarchs rise by virtue, or by sword?
Whoe'er grew great by keeping of his word?
Virtue 's a faint green-sickness to brave souls,
Dastards their hearts, their active heat controls.
The rival gods, monarchs of t' other world,
This mortal poison among princes hurled,
Fearing the mighty projects of the great
Should drive them from their proud celestial seat,
If not o'erawed by this new holy cheat.
Those pious frauds, too slight to ensnare the brave,
Are proper arts the long-eared rout to enslave.
Bribe hungry priests to deify your might,
To teach your will 's your only rule to right,
And sound damnation to all dare deny 't.
Thus Heaven's designs 'gainst Heaven you shall turn,
And make them fear those powers they once did scorn.
When all the gobbling interest of mankind,
By hirelings sold to you, shall be resigned,
And by impostures, God and man betrayed,
The church and state you safely may invade;
So boundless Lewis in full glory shines,
Whilst your starved power in legal fetters pines.
Shake off those baby-bands from your strong arms,
Henceforth be deaf to that old witch's charms;
Taste the delicious sweets of sovereign power,
'Tis royal game whole kingdoms to deflower.
Three spotless virgins to your bed I'll bring,
A sacrifice to you, their God and king.
As these grow stale, we'll harass human kind,
Rack nature, till new pleasures you shall find,
Strong as your reign, and beauteous as your mind.'

When she had spoke, a confused murmur rose,
Of French, Scotch, Irish, all my mortal foes;
Some English too, O shame! disguised I spied,
Led all by the wise son-in-law of Hyde.
With fury drunk, like bacchanals, they roar,
Down with that common Magna Charta whore!
With joint consent on helpless me they flew,
And from my Charles to a base gaol me drew;
My reverend age exposed to scorn and shame,
To prigs, bawds, whores, was made the public game.
Frequent addresses to my Charles I send,
And my sad state did to his care commend;
But his fair soul, transformed by that French dame,
Had lost all sense of honour, justice, fame.
Like a tame spinster in's seraigle he sits,
Besieged by whores, buffoons, and bastard chits;
Lulled in security, rolling in lust,
Resigns his crown to angel Carwell's trust;
Her creature O[sbor]ne the revenue steals;
False Finch, knave Anglesey misguide the seals.
Mac-James the Irish bigots does adore,
His French and Teague command on sea and shore.
The Scotch-scalado of our Court two isles,
False Lauderdale, with ordure, all defiles.
Thus the state 's nightmared by this hellish rout,
And no one left these furies to cast out.
Ah! Vindex come, and purge the poisoned state;
Descend, descend, ere the cure's desperate.

Raleigh   Once more, great queen, thy darling strive to save,
Snatch him again from scandal and the grave;
Present to 's thoughts his long-scorned Parliament,
The basis of his throne and government.
In his deaf ears sound his dead father's name;
Perhaps that spell may 's erring soul reclaim:
Who knows what good effects from thence may spring?
'Tis godlike good to save a falling king.

Britannia   Raleigh, no more, for long in vain I've tried
The Stuart from the tyrant to divide;
As easily learned virtuosos may

With the dog's blood his gentle kind convey
Into the wolf, and make him guardian turn
To the bleating flock, by him so lately torn:
If this imperial juice once taint his blood,
'Tis by no potent antidote withstood.
Tyrants, like leprous kings, for public weal
Should be immured, lest the contagion steal
Over the whole. The elect of the Jessean line
To this firm law their sceptre did resign;
And shall this base tyrannic brood invade
Eternal laws, by God for mankind made?
  To the serene Venetian state I'll go,
From her sage mouth famed principles to know;
With her the prudence of the ancients read,
To teach my people in their steps to tread;
By their great pattern such a state I'll frame,
Shall eternize a glorious lasting name.
Till then, my Raleigh, teach our noble youth
To love sobriety, and holy truth;
Watch and preside over their tender age,
Lest Court corruption should their souls engage;
Teach them how arts, and arms, in thy young days,
Employed our youth, – not taverns, stews, and plays;
Tell them the generous scorn their race does owe
To flattery, pimping, and a gaudy show;
Teach them to scorn the Carwells, Portsmouths, Nells,
The Clevelands, O[sbor]nes, Berties, Lauderdales:
Poppæa, Tigelline, and Asteria's name,
All yield to these in lewdness, lust, and fame.
Make them admire the Talbots, Sydneys, Veres,
Drake, Cavendish, Blake, men void of slavish fears,
True sons of glory, pillars of the state,
On whose famed deeds all tongues and writers wait.
When with fierce ardour their bright souls do burn,
Back to my dearest country I'll return.
Tarquin's just judge, and Cæsar's equal peers,
With them I'll bring to dry my people's tears;
Publicola with healing hands shall pour
Balm in their wounds, and shall their life restore;
Greek arts, and Roman arms, in her conjoined,

Shall England raise, relieve oppressed mankind.
As Jove's great son the infested globe did free
From noxious monsters, hell-born tyranny,
So shall my England, in a holy war,
In triumph lead chained tyrants from afar;
Her true Crusado shall at last pull down
The Turkish crescent and the Persian sun.
Freed by thy labours, fortunate, blest isle,
The earth shall rest, the Heaven shall on thee smile;
And this kind secret for reward shall give,
No poisonous serpent on the earth shall live.

On the Lord Mayor and Court of Aldermen

PRESENTING THE KING AND DUKE OF YORK
EACH WITH A COPY OF HIS FREEDOM,
ANNO DOM. 1674

A BALLAD

I

The Londoners gent
To the King do present,
In a box, the City maggot;
'Tis a thing full of weight,
That requires all the might
Of the whole Guildhall team to drag it.

II

Whilst their churches unbuilt,
And their houses undwelt,
And their orphans want bread to feed 'em;
Themselves they've bereft
Of the little wealth they had left,
To make an offering of the freedom.

III

O ye addle-brained cits!
Who, henceforth, in their wits,
Would entrust their youth to your heeding?
When in diamonds and gold
You have him thus enrolled,
Ye know both his friends and his breeding!

IV

Beyond the sea he began
Where such a riot he ran,
That every one there did leave him;
And now he's come o'er
Ten times worse than before,
When none but such fools would receive him.

V

He ne'er knew, not he,
How to serve or be free,
Though he has passed through so many adventures;
But e'er since he was bound,
(That is, he was crowned)
He has every day broke his indentures.

VI

He spends all his days
In running to plays,
When he ought in his shop to be poring;
And he wastes all his nights
In his constant delights,
Of revelling, drinking, and whoring.

VII

Throughout Lombard Street,
Each man did he meet,
He would run on the score with and borrow;
When they asked for their own,
He was broke and was gone,
And his creditors all left to sorrow.

VIII

Though oft bound to the peace,
Yet he never would cease
To vex his poor neighbours with quarrels;
And when he was beat,
He still made his retreat
To his Clevelands, his Nells, and his Carwells.

IX

Nay, his company lewd
Were twice grown so rude,
That had not fear taught him sobriety,
And the house being well barred,
With guard upon guard,
They'd robbed us of all our propriety.

X

Such a plot was laid,
Had not Ashley betrayed,
As had cancelled all former disasters;
And your wives had been strumpets
To his highness's trumpets,
And footboys had all been your masters.

XI

So many are the debts,
And the bastards he gets,
Which must all be defrayed by London;
That notwithstanding the care
Of Sir Thomas Player,
The chamber must needs be undone.

XII

His words nor his oath
Cannot bind him to troth,
And he values not credit or history;
And though he has served through
Two 'prenticeships now,
He knows not his trade nor his mystery.

XIII

Then, London, rejoice
In thy fortunate choice,
To have him made free of thy spices;
And do not mistrust,
He may once grow more just,
When he's worn off his follies and vices.

XIV

And what little thing
Is that which you bring
To the Duke, the kingdom's darling?
Ye hug it, and draw
Like ants at a straw,
Though too small for the gristle of starling.

XV

Is it a box of pills
To cure the Duke's ills?
He is too far gone to begin it!
Or does your fine show
In processioning go,
With the pyx and the host within it?

XVI

The very first head
Of the oath you him read,
Show you all how fit he 's to govern,
When in heart, you all knew,
He ne'er was, nor will be, true
To his country or to his sovereign.

XVII

And who, pray, could swear,
That he would forbear
To cull out the good of an alien,
Who still doth advance
The government of France
With a wife and religion Italian?

XVIII

And now, worshipful sirs,
Go, fold up your furs,
And Viners turn again, turn again;
I see (whoe'er's freed,)
You for slaves are decreed,
Until you burn again, burn again.

Nostradamus' Prophecy

For faults and follies London's doom shall fix;
And she must sink in flames in sixty-six.
Fire-balls shall fly, but few shall see the train,
As far as from Whitehall to Pudding Lane,
To burn the city, which again shall rise,
Beyond all hopes, aspiring to the skies,
Where vengeance dwells. But there is one thing more,
Though its walls stand, shall bring the city lower:
When legislators shall their trust betray,
Saving their own, shall give the rest away;
And those false men, by the easy people sent,
Give taxes to the King by Parliament;
When barefaced villains shall not blush to cheat,
And chequer-doors shall shut up Lombard Street;
When players come to act the part of queens,
Within the curtains, and behind the scenes;
When sodomy shall be prime minister's sport,
And whoring shall be the least crime at Court;
When boys shall take their sisters for their mate,
And practise incest between seven and eight;
When no man knows in whom to put his trust,
And e'en to rob the chequer shall be just;
When declarations, lies, and every oath,
Shall be in use at Court, but faith and troth;
When two good kings shall be at Brentford town,
And when in London there shall not be one;
When the seal 's given to a talking fool,
Whom wise men laugh at, and whom women rule,
A minister able only in his tongue,
To make harsh empty speeches two hours long;
When an old Scotch covenanter shall be
The champion for the English hierarchy;
When bishops shall lay all religion by,
And strive by law to establish tyranny;
When a lean treasurer shall in one year
Make himself fat, his King and people bare;
When the English prince shall Englishmen despise,

And think French only loyal, Irish wise;
When wooden shoon shall be the English wear,
And Magna Charta shall no more appear; –
Then the English shall a greater tyrant know,
Than either Greek or Latin story show;
Their wives to 's lust exposed, their wealth to 's spoil,
With groans, to fill his treasury, they toil;
But like the Bellides must sigh in vain,
For that still filled flows out as fast again;
Then they with envious eyes shall Belgium see,
And wish in vain Venetian liberty.
    The frogs too late, grown weary of their pain,
Shall pray to Jove to take him back again.

The Statue at Charing Cross

I

What can be the mystery? why Charing Cross
    This five months continues still muffled with board;
Dear Wheeler, impart, we are all at a loss,
    Unless we must have Punchinello restored.

II

'T were to Scaramouchio too great disrespect
    To limit his troop to this theatre small;
Besides the injustice it were to eject
    That mimic, so legally seized of Whitehall.

III

For a dial the place is too insecure,
    Since the Privy Garden could not it defend;
And so near to the Court they will never endure
    Any monument, how they their time may misspend.

IV

Were these deals yet in store for sheathing our fleet,
    When the King in armada to Portsmouth should sail,
On the Bishops and Treasurer, did they agree 't
    To repair with such riff-raff our church's old pale?

V

No; to comfort the heart of the poor cavalier,
 The late King on horseback is here to be shown;
What ado with your Kings and your statues is here!
 Have we not had enough, pray, already of one?

VI

Does the Treasurer think men so loyally tame,
 When their pensions are stopped, to be fooled with a
  sight?
And 'tis forty to one, if he play the old game,
 He'll reduce us ere long to rehearse forty-eight.

VII

The Trojan horse, so (not of brass, but of wood),
 Had within it an army that burned down the town;
However, 'tis ominous, if understood,
 For the old King on horseback is but an half-crown.

VIII

Yet, his brother-in-law's horse had gained such repute,
 That the Treasurer thought prudent to try it again;
And, instead of that market of herbs and of fruit,
 He will here keep a shambles of Parliament men.

IX

But why is the work then so long at a stand?
 Such things you should never, or suddenly do:
As the Parliament twice was prorogued by your hand,
 Would you venture so far to prorogue the King too?

X

Let 's have a King, sir, be he new, be he old,
 Not Viner delayed us so, though he were broken:
Though the King be of copper, and Danby of gold,
 Shall the Treasurer of guineas refuse such a token?

XI

The housewifery treasuress sure is grown nice,
 And so liberally treated the members at supper;
She thinks not convenient to go to the price,
 And we've lost both our King, and our horse, and his
  crupper.

XII

Where so many parties there are to provide,
   To buy a King is not so wise as to sell;
And however, she said, it could not be denied,
   That a monarch of gingerbread might do as well.

XIII

But the Treasurer told her he thought she was mad,
   And his Parliament list too withal did produce;
When he showed her, that so many voters he had,
   As would the next tax reimburse them with use.

XIV

So the statue will up after all this delay,
   But to turn the face towards Whitehall you must shun;
Though of brass, yet with grief it would melt him away
   To behold such a prodigal Court and a son.

A Dialogue between Two Horses

THE INTRODUCTION

We read, in profane and sacred records,
Of beasts which have uttered articulate words:
When magpies and parrots cry, *walk, knaves, walk!*
It is a clear proof that birds too may talk;
And statues, without either windpipes or lungs,
Have spoken as plainly as men do with tongues.
Livy tells a strange story, can hardly be fellowed,
That a sacrificed ox, when his guts were out, bellowed;
Phalaris had a bull, which grave authors tell ye,
Would roar like a devil with a man in his belly;
Friar Bacon had a head that spake made of brass;
And Balaam the prophet was reproved by his ass;
At Delphos and Rome stocks and stones, now and then, sirs,
Have to questions returned articulate answers.
All Popish believers think something divine,

When images speak, possesseth the shrine;
But they that faith catholic ne'er understood,
When shrines give an answer, a knave's on the rood.
Those idols ne'er spoke, but are miracles done
By the devil, a priest, a friar, or a nun.
If the Roman church, good Christians, oblige ye
To believe man and beast have spoke in effigy,
Why should we not credit the public discourses
In a dialogue between two inanimate horses?
The horses I mean of Wool-Church and Charing,
Who told many truths worth any man's hearing,
Since Viner and Osborne did buy and provide 'em
For the two mighty monarchs who now do bestride 'em.
The stately brass stallion and the white marble steed
One night came together, by all 'tis agreed;
When both Kings were weary of sitting all day,
Were stolen off, incognito, each his own way;
And then the two jades, after mutual salutes,
Not only discoursed, but fell to disputes.

THE DIALOGUE

Quoth the marble horse,

Wool-Church It would make a stone speak,
To see a Lord Mayor and a Lombard Street break,
Thy founder and mine to cheat one another,
When both knaves agreed to be each other's brother. –

Here Charing broke forth, and thus he went on:

Charing My brass is provokèd as much as thy stone,
To see church and state bow down to a whore,
And the King's chief minister holding the door;
The money of widows and orphans employed,
And the bankers quite broke to maintain the whore's
pride.

Wool-Church To see Dei Gratia writ on the throne,
And the King's wicked life say, God there is none.

Charing That he should be styled Defender of the Faith,
Who believes not a word what the Word of God saith.

Wool-Church   That the Duke should turn papist, and that Church defy
            For which his own father a martyr did die.

Charing   Though he changed his religion, I hope he's so civil
            Not to think his own father is gone to the devil.

Wool-Church   That bondage and beggary should be in a nation
            By a cursed House of Commons, and a blessed
                 Restoration.

Charing   To see a white staff make a beggar a lord,
            And scarce a wise man at a long council-board.

Wool Church   That the Bank should be seized, yet the 'Chequer so
                 poor,
            'Lord have mercy!' and a cross may be set on the door.

Charing   That a million and half should be the revenue,
            Yet the King of his debts pay no man a penny.

Wool-Church   That a King should consume three kingdoms' estates,
            And yet all the Court be as poor as church rats.

Charing   That of four seas dominion, and of all their guarding,
            No token should appear, but a poor copper farthing.

Wool- Church Our worm-eaten ships to be laid up at Chatham,
            Not our trade to secure, but for fools to come at 'em.

Charing   And our few ships abroad become Tripoli's scorn,
            By pawning for victuals their guns at Leghorn.

Wool-Church   That making us slaves by horse and foot guard,
            For restoring the King, shall be all our reward.

Charing   The basest ingratitude ever was heard!
            But tyrants ungrateful are always afeared.

Wool-Church   On Harry the Seventh's head he that placèd the crown
            Was after rewarded by losing his own.

Charing   That Parliament-men should rail at the Court,
            And get good preferments immediately for 't;
            To see them that suffered for father and son,
            And helpèd to bring the latter to his throne,
            That with lives and estates did loyally serve,

And yet for all this can nothing deserve;
The King looks not on 'em, preferments denied 'em,
The Roundheads insult, and the courtiers deride 'em,
And none get preferments, but who will betray
Their country to ruin; 'tis that opes the way
Of the bold-talking members.

Wool-Church   If the bastards you add,
What a number of rascally lords have been made.

Charing   That traitors to the country, in a bribed House of
      Commons,
Should give away millions at every summons.

Wool-Church   Yet some of those givers, such beggarly villains,
As not to be trusted for twice fifty shillings.

Charing   No wonder that beggars should still be for giving,
Who out of what's given do get a good living.

Wool-Church   Four knights and a knave, who were burgesses made,
For selling their consciences were liberally paid.

Charing   How base are the souls of such low-prizèd sinners,
Who vote with the Court for drink and for dinners!

Wool-Church   'Tis they who brought on us this scandalous yoke,
Of excising our cups, and taxing our smoke.

Charing   But thanks to the whores who made the King doggèd,
For giving no more the rogues are proroguèd.

Wool-Church   That a King should endeavour to make a war cease,
Which augments and secures his own profit and peace.

Charing   And plenipotentiaries sent into France,
With an addle-headed knight, and a lord without brains.

Wool-Church   That the King should send for another French whore,
When one already had made him so poor.

Charing   The misses take place, each advanced to be duchess,
With pomp great as queens in their coach and six
      horses;
Their bastards made dukes, earls, viscounts, and lords,
And all the high titles that honour affords.

Wool-Church	While these brats and their mothers do live in such plenty,
	The nation's impoverished, and the 'Chequer quite empty;
	And though war was pretended when the money was lent,
	More on whores, than in ships or in war, hath been spent.
Charing	Enough, my dear brother, although we speak reason,
	Yet truth many times being punished for treason,
	We ought to be wary, and bridle our tongue,
	Bold speaking hath done both men and beasts wrongs.
	When the ass so boldly rebukèd the prophet,
	Thou knowest what danger had like to come of it;
	Though the beast gave his master ne'er an ill word,
	Instead of a cudgel, Balaam wished for a sword.
Wool-Church	Truth 's as bold as a lion, I am not afraid;
	I'll prove every tittle of what I have said.
	Our riders are absent, who is 't that can hear?
	Let's be true to ourselves, whom then need we fear?
	Where is thy King gone?
Charing	To see Bishop Laud.
Wool-Church	Mine to cuckold a scrivener's in masquerade;
	For on such occasions he oft strays away,
	And returns to remount me about break of day.
	In very dark nights sometimes you may find him,
	With a harlot got up on my crupper behind him.
Charing	Pause, brother, awhile, and calmly consider
	What thou hast to say against my royal rider.
Wool-Church	Thy priest-ridden King turned desperate fighter
	For the surplice, lawn-sleeves, the cross, and the mitre;
	Till at last on the scaffold he was left in the lurch,
	By knaves, who cried up themselves for the church.
Charing	Archbishops and bishops, archdeacons and deans!
	Thy King will ne'er fight unless 't be for his queens.
Wool-Church	He that dies for ceremonies, dies like a fool.

Charing   The King on thy back is a lamentable tool.

Wool-Church The goat and the lion I equally hate,
        And freemen alike value life and estate;
        Though the father and son be different rods,
        Between the two scourgers we find little odds;
        Both infamous stand in three kingdoms' votes,
        This for picking our pockets, that for cutting our throats.

Charing   More tolerable are the lion-king's slaughters,
        Than the goat making whores of our wives and our
            daughters;
        The debauchèd and cruel, since they equally gall us,
        I had rather bear Nero than Sardanapalus.

Wool-Church One of the two tyrants must still be our case,
        Under all who shall reign of the false Stuart's race.
        De Witt and Cromwell had each a brave soul,
        I freely declare it, I am for old Noll;
        Though his government did a tyrant resemble,
        He made England great, and his enemies tremble.

Charing   Thy rider puts no man to death in his wrath,
        But is buried alive in lust and in sloth.

Wool-Church What is thy opinion of James, Duke of York?

Charing   The same that the frogs had of Jupiter's stork.
        With the Turk in his head, and the Pope in his heart,
        Father Patrick's disciples will make England smart.
        If e'er he be King, I know Britain's doom,
        We must all to a stake, or be converts to Rome.
        Ah, Tudor! ah, Tudor! we have had Stuarts enough;
        None ever reigned like old Bess in the ruff.
        Her Walsingham could dark counsels unriddle,
        And our Sir Joseph write news, books, and fiddle.

Wool-Church Truth, brother, well said; but that's somewhat bitter;
        His perfumed predecessor was never more fitter:
        Yet we have one Secretary honest and wise;
        For that very reason, he's never to rise.
        But canst thou devise when things will be mended?

Charing   When the reign of the line of the Stuarts is ended.

Conclusion   If speeches from animals in Rome's first age
Prodigious events did surely presage,
That should come to pass, all mankind may swear
That which two inanimate horses declare.
But I should have told you, before the jades parted,
Both galloped to Whitehall, and there humbly farted;
Which tyranny's downfall portended much more,
Than all that the beasts had spoken before.
If the Delphic Sibyl's oracular speeches
(As learned men say) came out of their breeches,
Why might not our horses, since words are but wind,
Have the spirit of prophecy likewise behind?
Though tyrants make laws, which they strictly proclaim,
To conceal their own faults and to cover their shame,
Yet the beasts in the field, and the stones in the wall,
Will punish their faults and prophesy their fall;
When they take from the people the freedom of words,
They teach them the sooner to fall to their swords.
Let the city drink coffee and quietly groan,
They who conquered the father won't be slaves to the
    son.
For wine and strong drink make tumults increase,
Chocolate, tea, and coffee are liquors of peace;
No quarrels or oaths are among those who drink 'em,
'Tis Bacchus and the brewer swear, *damn 'em!* and
    sink 'em!
Then, Charles, thy late edict against coffee recall,
There's ten times more treason in brandy and ale.

INDEX OF POEM TITLES

INDEX OF FIRST LINES